THE HOOSIER HOT SHOTS

AND MY FRIEND GABE

By Dick Stodghill

JLT – CHARATAN PUBLICATIONS

ISBN: 978-0-6151-7517-1
JLT – CHARATAN PUBLICATIONS

For Gabe, Ken and Hezzie, a trio of young Hoosier boys who set out from the plains of Central Indiana with little more than their love of music, people, and a bit of fun. And to Jackie, whose help and encouragement makes all things possible.

ACKNOWLEDGEMENTS

Without the letters and tapes sent to me by Gabe Ward this book could not have been written. They provided a bonanza of information about the Hoosier Hot Shots, some of it conflicting with stories previously accepted as factual. How the Hot Shots got their name and the recording of *Someday*, for example. Gabe had no idea the material would eventually end up in a book. Had he known, he would have been pleased. I'm sure his longtime friends, Ken and Hezzie Trietsch, would have felt the same.

There are other sources of information about the Hot Shots, Gennett Records, radio station WLS and the National Barn Dance that were most helpful. They can be found in the bibliography and most of them are on the Internet.

A true storehouse of information is available at The Hoosier Hot Shots Museum website. Anyone who enjoys this book will love www.hoosierhotshots.com

For information on Hot Shot material available for purchase, call up www.hezzie.com

There are other sites, many of them, to be found by Googling Hoosier Hot Shots. None can equal the two mentioned above, but some are of interest and provide elusive bits of information.

Photo of Gabe and Dick on page 123, credit Jackie Stodghill.

And finally, John Carlson of the Star Press in Muncie verified that the Trietsch brothers were not born in Delaware County as their obituaries reported.

CONTENTS

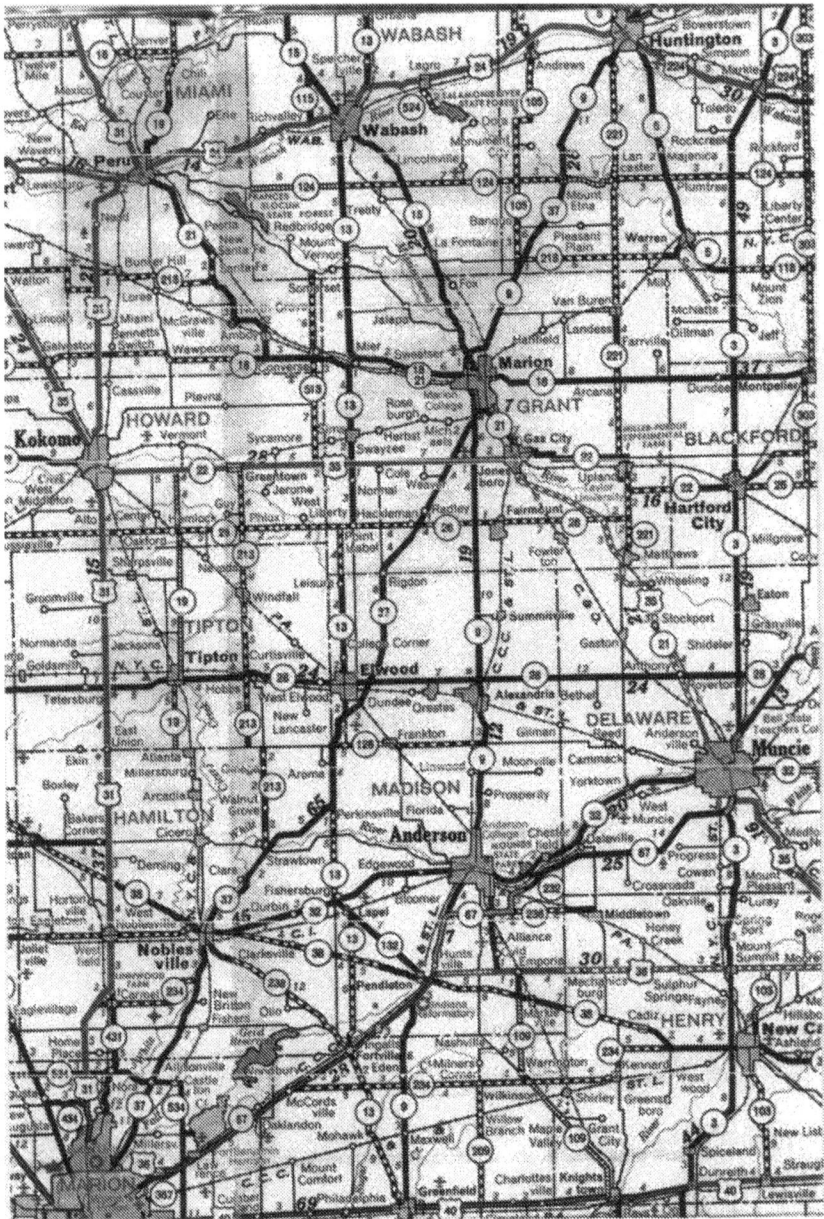

Home Country for the Hoosier Hot Shots: Eaton, Cowan, Knightstown, Arcadia, Alexandria, Elwood and Muncie played key roles during their formative years as well as their future development and careers.

PROLOGUE

Time has slipped by, the world has changed and the boys are gone now, so where can we find the Hoosier Hot Shots today? In closing countless stage shows, Hezzie told us the way:

You simply turn to the right at the crossroads,
And then turn left at the little red barn,
Turn down the lane of memories,
Gaze at the stars that used to be,
Then go straight down the pathway of childhood,
Where the red leaves of dreams tumble down.
Though you arrive, just in imagination,
We'll all greet you at the station,
In our town – everyone's home town.
That's it.

An audio tape sent to me by Gabe Ward in the late 1980s included Hezzie's standard routine for closing Hot Shot stage performances. After telling a few unsophisticated jokes and repeating what a wonderful audience they had been several times he would say how much the boys enjoyed their visit and hoped everyone would come by to see them some time. Then came the above words followed by everyone joining in on a rousing finale.

When it ended, Gabe laughed for a moment before saying, "Can you imagine somebody making a living today off that kind of stuff?"

Yes, Gabe, many of us can. He didn't live long enough to see the Internet with its thousands of listings for the Hot Shots including the wonderful Hoosier Hot Shots Museum site. He would have loved that, just as Ken and Hezzie would have, and all of them would be thrilled to know their songs are available now on compact discs. Nearly all their movies can be found on the web, too. I don't believe they expected to be remembered after the passage of so much time.

The story of the Hoosier Hot Shots is truly a Horatio Alger tale of hard work leading to success. I told some of it in columns written for the Muncie Evening Press. The first of them brought a note from Gabe, a prolific writer of letters, and for the remainder of his life we engaged in a voluminous correspondence. His final letter was written two days before his death in 1992. We met face to face only once, yet I grew to consider this friendly, outgoing man a close friend. In one column I wrote: "I have never met or corresponded with a man of such amazing optimism or one so completely unspoiled by success. A letter from Gabe never fails to make me feel a little better about the world."

Residents of the Muncie area enjoyed reading Gabe's letters as much as I did. No wonder; two of the three original Hoosier Hot Shots, Ken and Hezzie Trietsch, were local boys and Gabe had grown up in nearby Alexandria and Elwood. I'm not sure Gabe realized just how much material he supplied for me over the years. Or to put it another way, how much easier he made it for someone required to crank out five 750-word columns every week.

More often than not Gabe's letters contained enclosures – tapes of Hot Shot recordings, photos, old playbills and newspaper clippings. Along with the songs he always had stories to tell. A tape enclosed with his last letter included a recording he had made just that morning.

The Hoosier Hot Shots played down-home music, that no one can deny. Classifying them as simply a novelty band would be a mistake, though. The boys were true jazz musicians although they never wanted to stray too far from their basic routines so that aspect of their talent was seldom apparent to listeners. They also could play it straight when the mood or the need arose. But their roots were in vaudeville so entertaining an audience was their top priority. That, and having fun, the kind that could be shared with listeners.

Gabe expressed it this way: "Even on radio we always treated it like we had on vaudeville, doing our act with all the movement and action. We always imagined we had an audience sitting out front."

I learned a great deal about Ken and Hezzie from those letters and tapes from Gabe. He often wrote and spoke of their years with the Ezra Buzzington Rube Band on vaudeville and then the forming of the group that came to be known as the Hoosier Hot Shots. Through it all – radio stardom, recording contracts, movies in Hollywood, television – the boys remained what they had been at the beginning, three friendly, unspoiled fellows from the flatland farm country of Central Indiana.

Although she was from a small Ohio town, the same was true of Gabe's wife, Marguerite. They were married in 1928 so she had been through it all with them, both the good times and the bad. None of it ever changed them; to the very end they remained an unaffected Hoosier boy and Buckeye girl. Gabe called her, "My American Express – I won't leave home without her."

A unique twosome, Marguerite and Gabe Ward. A pair who never, as the years passed by, found time to grow old. The same was true of Gabe's close friends of six decades, Ken Trietsch and the brother he so often turned to and said, "Are you ready, Hezzie?"   – DS

In the Press of things

By DICK STODGHILL

Can someone give him inside dope on Hoosier Hot Shots?

Whatever happened to the Hoosier Hot Shots? And "Take it away, Rosedale."

This comes to mind because another season is ending and once again I didn't get to see the Rosedale Hot Shots in action. That and seeing a game in that round gymnasium at Frankfort are two of my more important goals in life.

The Hoosier Hot Shots were big in the early days of radio. Everyone tuned in the bulky old Grunow over in the corner of the living room or the Philco table model and listened to "In a Little Red Barn on a Farm Down in Indiana." Now you have to get up with the birds if you want to hear a barbershop quartet version on WOWO in Fort Wayne. I like it, but not that much.

Actually I don't know anything about the Hoosier Hot Shots but I'd like to. Who were they? Where were they from? Probably Peoria or Dubuque. And who was that guy who said, "Take it away, Rosedale?" I think they called him Uncle Ezra.

In the unlikely event that someone doesn't know, Rosedale is a town of 817 on the banks of Big Raccoon Creek. It's not too far from Terre Haute, which means it also isn't too far from Toad Hop, and Clinton is just a few miles to the west. The Hot Shots of Rosedale seldom leap to mind when asked to name the powers of Indiana basketball, but the name has a nice ring to it.

Another favorite of the Hoosier Hot Shots was "I Wish That I Was Back in Indiana," a tune not to be confused with others having similar names. That, I'm sorry to say, is everything I know about Rosedale, the Rosedale Hot Shots, and the Hoosier Hot Shots. Experience tells me, though, that someone in Muncie hails from Rosedale and someone else knows all about the quartet, assuming it was a quartet.

WHO WERE THOSE HOT SHOTS?

What can be said about that column on the opposite page? For starters, it might have been worded a bit more thoughtfully and I should have made a few inquiries before sitting down to write. That part in the middle, for example: *Actually I don't know anything about the Hoosier Hot Shots but I'd like to. Who were they? Where were they from? Probably Peoria or Dubuque.*

There were several things wrong with those four sentences. I did know something about the Hot Shots, having grown up listening to them on the National Barn Dance most Saturday evenings. Later I occasionally heard them on jukeboxes when someone else dropped a nickel in the slot. I was too tight with my money to throw it away like that. Then I saw them in a couple of movies that were second billing on a double feature. I was there to see the other film but enjoyed the antics of the boys.

The most jarring error was the matter of location. My column ran five days a week in the Muncie Evening Press. That clipping is just the first half of one of the 2,500 I wrote between 1980 and 1990. It was a popular feature of the paper if I do say so myself. In 1981 it won an award as Best Column In Indiana from United Press International (UPI).

Why does that enter into the picture? Because none of the three core members of the Hoosier Hot Shots were from Peoria or Dubuque. Two grew up on a farm seven miles south of Muncie. The third spent most of his boyhood nineteen miles away in Alexandria, the rest a few miles farther down the road in Elwood.

Oh, boy! Did the good folks of Muncie ever put me wise. For days the newsroom phones seldom stopped ringing. The mailman was ready to demand an assistant if the avalanche of letters didn't subside. Other reporters banged out their copy and left as quickly as possible, fed up with taking calls meant for me.

Then came the capper, a letter from one of the two original Hot Shots still living. That, of course, was Gabe Ward. A decade-long friendship began at that moment. We met face to face only a single time but our voluminous correspondence created a bond that continued right up to Gabe's death. He often included tapes of Hot Shots music and his own comments that were easier said into a microphone than put on paper, although Gabe loved to write letters.

His last letter was written just two days before he died. Enclosed was a tape containing a newly-recorded clarinet solo of *Back Home Again In Indiana*. If ever a song came from the heart, this was it – a slow nostalgic look back to a better and happier time. Gabe never lost his deep and abiding love for the state where he was born and raised and the stories he told of growing up in Alexandria and Elwood would fill a book. Too bad he never wrote it, and too bad I didn't write this one twenty years earlier. Gabe would have loved knowing there was a book devoted to the Hoosier Hot Shots. He would be thrilled, too, over the number of the group's songs now available on compact discs. Above all, though, he could have answered some of the questions that arose during this writing.

During the course of a long and eventful life I have known, met or interviewed a countless number of men – politicians, entertainers, famous athletes, soldiers and just ordinary Joes. Not one of them came close to Gabe Ward for sheer, unfailing optimism. No matter how painful an event, and he had a number of them in his late years, Gabe could always find some glimmer of hope, of cheer, of cause to pick up his clarinet and express himself in the music he so dearly loved. A wonderful man, Gabe Ward.

And talented. And humorous. In a letter written to me on June 15, 1987 he said: "Over the years I've been asked why I didn't get an up to date improved system (clarinet). Some indicated I might have been fairly great on the clarinet if I had studied!" He signed the letter, "Ol' System Gabe."

Old system or new, Gabe was a great clarinet player and there was nothing "fairly" about it. That was also true of his down-home Hoosier humor. Dry, often self-deprecating, but

14

always evident. He could make beautiful music on a saxophone, too.

Charles Otto Ward was born November 26, 1904 in Knightstown, a small town on U.S. 40, the National Road, about 35 miles east of Indianapolis. Midway between the two is Greenfield, home of Hoosier poet James Whitcomb Riley. Gabe started school in Indianapolis and it was there that Riley visited his classroom one memorable day. Hard as it might be to believe in the 21st century, Gabe had to study German in the first grade.

In his birthplace, Knightstown, those who watched the Gene Hackman movie *Hoosiers* saw the gym in the old Knightstown High School. In the film it was the home of the fictitious Hickory High basketball team.

The Ward's stay in Indianapolis was brief so Gabe was still quite young when the family moved north to the small town of Alexandria. The local newspaper, the Times-Tribune, had a slogan: "Alexandria - Not on the Nile, but just as worthwhile." Gabe said it could also be seen on signs at the city limits. He spent the remainder of his elementary school days there. Not only was his memory of those years remarkable, his letters provide a word picture of a life completely alien to Americans today. Here are a few excerpts:

"June 11th I started some repair work on my very first clarinet – a 13 key, 2 ring High

OTTO AT AGE FOUR

Pitch from France. My Uncle Dewey Ward played it in the Indianapolis News Boys band in 1909-10-11. He brought it to me in Alexandria in 1917. It hung in our coal shed for a year

15

before I found I could get some instruction at the high school – 35 cents per lesson – and   I became really interested. In six months I was on 3rd clarinet on easy stuff. Then I began to love the old clarinet. . ."

"The past 20 months have allowed me to a do a whole bunch of serious thinking along with that same old line that permeates my body 'n' soul from as far back as I can remember. I love today but I love to recall the times that I carried wood 'n' coal to build a fire for Daddy Phillips at the big school on the hill at Innisdale. He was a kind 'n' gentle pot-bellied man who could blow a mean pitch pipe to start our school day with *Flow Gently Sweet Afton* or *Columbia The Gem Of The Ocean,* a flag salute, a prayer and then some education! Four grades in the big school room, four in the little school about three blocks away.

"Stella Pentecost Ward from the town and covered bridge area of Matthews was a well known mother and sometimes mid-wife, wet nurse and beloved by all of mankind. Kids got satisfaction from that lady when they needed it! She was our Mother – uneducated basically but surely 'A Saint.'

"I like to sit 'n' think about life in a 3 room house with a summer kitchen, 3 lots of garden, toilet out back or in a secluded corner of a room, a dug well, frozen pump and handle, some manure around the house's foundation to help insulate, long stockings over our shoes to trudge about a mile thru the snow to school. A foot log across Pipe Creek on the way to downtown Alexandria.

"I met old man Sawyer who invented Rock Wool from Indiana limestone in his quarry. Dad Ward wheeled that stone up ramps at $1.75 per ten hour day! He let me have fire wood from his Mineral Wool factory.

"I lied about my age, at 13 I was big 'n' strong enough to work at Lippincott's Glass & Chimney factory at Alexandria. I was supposed to be 14 yrs. old. (Made) 55 cents for each 4 hours work or $6.05 for a week's work. Too much! Mother got it all but $1.00. She washed 'n' ironed for the Jimmy Wales family - $1.25 for both. He was mayor of Alexandria and a distant 2nd or 3rd cousin. We could get by O.K. Went to 1st Christian Church.

"I made a few bucks with the old $35 clarinet and selling newspapers. The weekly Saturday Blade and Chicago Ledger and Lone Scout magazine were good for about four dollars a week – 1917-19. I delivered Dr. Miles Almanac door to door for years! I liked to walk into the pressroom and gab. I came out with some nice space for the Hoosier Hot Shots by doing that. I still hear from a few old operators (in 1990).

"I could write volumes about Anderson, Muncie, Daleville, Marion, Fairmount, Summitville, Warsaw and the lakes, Elwood, Tipton, Noblesville, Cicero."

Many of us wish you had, Gabe.

A testament to Gabe's memory came late in the 1980s when the librarian in Alexandria, Elverda Songer, ordered a Hoosier Hot Shots tape from him. He enclosed a letter mentioning former schoolmates Marshall Broyles, Ruby Rutledge, Roxy Frazier, Donald Duncan, John Turgl, Mildred Dunn, Alpha Day, Chet Thomas, Thelma Howerton, Lenore and Ariel Brattain, the Fleenor twins and Ivan tootin' his horn as well as Professor Stoler.

He remembered the stores, too – Brown's Grocery, Neidi's Cigar Store, Bill Lipp's Theatre, and Broyle's Department Store. It was at Broyle's where his mother bought him his first pair of long pants, blue serge for $5.95. This came after Gabe found a dollar bill wrapped around a five dollar bill on the sidewalk.

In the letter Gabe also mentioned the job at Lippincott's, where he would carry in glass to the blowers and then take the finished products to the tempering ovens. He used some of the money he earned to take Thelma Culbertson to The Sugar Bowl to buy tin roof sundaes.

It didn't take the youthful Gabe – he was known as Otto at the time – long to get truly serious about music and he organized his own band shortly after the First World War ended in Europe. He wrote this about it:

"My Hoosier Melody Five was an attraction with *Roses of Picardy, Keep The Home Fires Burning, K-K-K-Katy* – of course *Alexander's Ragtime Band* and *Over There* never left the charts. To do a gig all summer at the Kosciusko County lakes at $25 a week plus room and board was absolutely tops.

To own a saxophone in 1920-24 was really big 'n' wild. People were wanting saxophones – boy was I glad I had a C-melody and could play from sheet music without transposing."

Among the places where the Hoosier Melody Five played was the upstairs Eagles lodge in Alexandria. There they made $3 a night. Gabe said the band did a lot of practicing but needed to know only twenty songs or so to play at dances. Considering the young age of the leader, who had taken lessons for only six months, it's surprising that the piano player was a 35-year-old graduate of a music conservatory. Rounding out the Hoosier Melody Five were a banjo, drums and fiddle with Gabe on the clarinet and saxophone.

For more than a century going "up to the lakes" has been a favorite summer pastime for residents of East Central Indiana. When they speak of "the lakes" they mean those in the vicinity of Syracuse, North Webster and Warsaw. It was natural for Otto to gravitate to the area, but considering he was only fifteen- or sixteen-years-old for him to have obtained a summer-long booking for his band is remarkable. Twenty-five dollars a week split five ways may not seem like much money today, but in Otto's time $5 on top of room and board was not to be sneezed at. As the leader he may have taken a slightly larger share for himself, of course. Yet knowing him, he may not.

The largest of the lakes, Wawasee, has always been the most prestigious place to own a cottage. In the old days staying at the large hotel on its shore stamped a man and his family as even more successful than the cottage dwellers. Next in line comes Tippecanoe and then a dozen or more smaller lakes, each with its own devotees.

So young Otto – soon to be Gabe – was busy making money, having fun and enjoying life. "My instinct told me I should always look and act happy," he said. That would never change over the next 70 years. His instinct served him well.

THE DAY BILL WHITEHURST BROKE HIS ARM

It would be just another long day in the classroom, or so thought Charles Otto Ward as he trudged along on his daily walk to Elwood High School at the edge of the downtown business district. Like most boys, young Otto, as he preferred to be called, could have named a dozen other ways he would rather have spent the next six or seven hours on that Friday in October of 1923.

Otto wasn't aware – and it might not have meant a thing to him even if he had been – that thirty miles away in Muncie, Bill Whitehurst was nursing a broken arm. It's possible, though, that he knew Whitehurst played clarinet in Ezra Buzzington's Rube Band. Music, particularly when played on a clarinet, was Otto's great passion in life. Already he had gained a reputation as one of Elwood's talented young people and a leader of his own band.

Elwood lies in the heart of the Central Indiana flatlands and that means tomato, corn and soybean country. In Otto's day the town spread out from east to west along State Route 28 so you might say it had more width than height. The highway follows a straight line for much of the time as it crosses that part of the state. A driver can travel for miles with little to do other than enjoy the scenery and move the steering wheel an inch or two now and then.

Back when Otto was a schoolboy the fields bounded by fencerows were not as large as they are today. The woods of oaks, maples and sycamores were always visible somewhere in the distance and the family farmhouses, barns and outbuildings were seldom spaced too far apart. There were cows in the pastures, hogs in the pens, chickens running freely around the barnyard and sometimes out on the road. A traveler on Route 28 would pass scattered villages off to the north and south of the highway and rare indeed was one without a grain elevator, silos and a feed store. He wouldn't be delayed too long in passing through the small towns of Alexandria, Elwood and

Tipton unless a slow Pennsylvania Railroad freight train was creeping along the tracks bisecting downtown Elwood. Approaching the business district from the south meant crossing the Nickel Plate Road's right-of-way and Union Traction had interurban tracks in Elwood. For a town its size, rail traffic was brisk.

A farm family or workers at the tinplate factory could find just about anything needed at the downtown Elwood stores. If not there, then certainly in the Sears-Roebuck catalog found in nearly every home. When something out of the ordinary was required in a hurry it could always be found in Anderson, the county seat.

That was a bit of a sore point with some people in Elwood even though Anderson was much larger. Just to the west, Tipton was considerably smaller than Elwood and yet it was a county seat with a courthouse on the town square. That rankled the leading citizens and the elected officials in Elwood, so they built a city hall almost as large and impressive as the courthouses in some small counties.

There was enough in the way of entertainment for the townspeople and those from nearby farms because people accustomed to working from sunup to sundown seldom had a need for it. When they did there were baseball games pitting the town's ball club against those from other Hoosier communities. In winter there were high school basketball games, sometimes with schools from as far away as Wabash or Peru. Now and then the local high school boys would even take on a team from one of the area's big cities – Marion, Kokomo or Muncie.

On a cold November night in 1943 my father, my Uncle Paul and I attended a game pitting the Muncie Central Bearcats against the Elwood Panthers. I had already been inducted into the Army but wouldn't report for a few more days. Muncie won, which was no surprise, yet the irate Elwood fans began turning over cars with out-of-county license plates. Fortunately we had parked a block away. The three of us beat a hasty retreat to a nearby bar until the excitement died down.

In the summer a carnival would set up in Elwood or a circus would visit Anderson, but the really big event of the year

20

was the Madison County Fair. Area farmers would enter their livestock in the competitions and Elwood boys and girls competed in various events with those from Summitville, Lapel, Pendleton and the many other small communities in the county. If one fair wasn't enough to satisfy folks in Elwood there was another nearby, the Tipton County Fair only a few miles to the west.

Elwood's biggest day came in 1940 when Wendell Willkie, the Republican candidate for president, gave his acceptance speech there. A crowd of 100,000 jammed the city streets. A native of Elwood, Willkie lost the election to Roosevelt.

For those with a taste for something a bit more sedate and quiet there were church suppers, ice cream socials, club and lodge meetings at the Odd Fellows Hall and similar places. Silent movies at the theater, too, and quite often live performances on stage by local residents with varying degrees of talent. Frequently professional entertainers would come to town – comedians, singers, bands of various size and musical ability.

That's where Bill Whitehurst's broken arm entered the picture.

Mark Schaefer and his zany bunch of musicians in Ezra Buzzington's Rube Band were booked for a weekend of performances at Elwood's Classic Theatre. For them the loss of Whitehurst was a catastrophe. He was the only member of the band sometimes referred to as the Rustic Revelers who bothered to play the melody. To the others it was just, well, something that shouldn't interfere with the fun or running off a few jazz riffs. There wouldn't be much of either, however, for the band's remaining sidemen at the time, Guy Merrill and the four Trietsch brothers, unless someone carried the tune.

What was to be done? The situation was desperate so Mark Schaefer made a few quick inquiries around town. As a result the members of the band, all of them, marched into Elwood High School at 11 o'clock in the morning. The problem was explained to those in authority and a lad who played clarinet was summoned from his classroom.

That lad was Otto Ward. Rather than spending the afternoon in class as he had expected, he put in two hard hours rehearsing the songs scheduled for the weekend. That evening he was playing the melody and performing solos at the Classic. He did such a fine job of it that he became a fixture with the band and a lengthy career in music was launched. When the Buzzington band moved on to its next engagement in Danville, Illinois, Otto went along.

Having bigger and better thing to occupy his time, Otto never returned to school. As time passed, being a dropout didn't bother him. He wrote this in 1988: "Nothing much has been written to praise high school dropouts but I can truthfully say plenty of opportunity exists for those with enough ambition and willingness to do the hard work to find decent companions and always save a few dimes."

Many other successful people could echo those words.

Whatever became of Bill Whitehurst? Many years later no one in Muncie, his hometown, seemed to know. Sixty-three years after that day in 1923, Otto, by then known as Gabe for so long his real name seldom came to mind, wished he knew the answer. "I'd love to know and I'd love to thank him for it all," wrote Gabe. "And of course I hope his arm is perfect. I never played as well as Bill."

There are those who would disagree with that last statement even though they never heard Bill Whitehurst perform. Expressing the thought was typical of Gabe, however..

There is cause to wonder if many modern day educators would be as wise as those in Elwood or would they contend that classroom work is far more important than playing in a band? It's possible, of course, that Gabe would have found his way to the Buzzington band at a later date had he been denied the opportunity that fateful day. There is an even greater possibility that he would not. Had that been the case, and if Bill Whitehurst hadn't broken his arm, there would have been no Hoosier Hot Shots, at least not as the country came to know them. Nor would this book have been written.

THE TRIETSCH BROTHERS

In his new role with the Buzzington band, Otto Ward soon found a couple of friends about his own age, Kenneth and Paul Trietsch. They were among four brothers in the band. The other two left the group so by the mid-1920s Ken and Paul along with Otto were the core elements.

The Trietsch boys were Central Indiana Hoosiers through and through. In their very young years the family of Henry and Emma Trietsch lived on a farm near Arcadia, a tiny community along the road leading from Noblesville, the county seat, north to Tipton. Ken was born there September 13, 1903, Paul on April 11,1905.

Big families were the norm in farm country at the time, what with cows to milk and a host of other chores waiting to be done every morning. It wasn't at all unusual that Henry and Emma had four daughters and five sons, but the family was different in one respect: they never allowed work to push music too far into the background.

A relative gave the Trietsches an old tuba and 5-year-old Ken quickly latched onto it. Before long he was able to play tunes, as far as it is possible to play them on a tuba, and as time went along he became proficient on a variety of instruments.

Chores he wasn't too crazy about led Paul to music. He had to help his mother with the Monday washing, an onerous task he livened up by whistling and strumming tunes on her washboard. Some might have said he was merely making an unseemly amount of noise but fortunately there were no neighbors close by to complain.

Another job was bringing the cows home from pasture in the evening. An imaginative boy, Paul realized the bells around the neck of each cow were making what might pass for music, at least for someone with a tin ear. That was not true of Paul, however, so by adding cowbells to the washboard he was making louder if not better music. Over time he added horns, whistles and other noise makers to the contraption but also was developing some skill on more conventional instruments.

For a brief time the family moved south, living in Alabama and Georgia, but soon returned to Indiana and settled on a farm about seven miles south of Muncie. The children attended school in the nearby hamlet of Cowan. Paul played basketball on the Cowan High team while Ken was winning prizes at the Delaware County Fair for the corn he had raised. He also was playing in a local band.

The five Trietsch boys gained a bit of notoriety by taking part in a local minstrel show in which they used a variety of musical instruments highlighted by Paul's washboard, his "Monday Morning Piana." So well received was this that the elder Trietsch, a skilled performer on the banjo, organized the Trietsch Family Band and obtained bookings on both American and Canadian vaudeville circuits. There were numerous circuits at the time, some large and some small. It is doubtful that the band played on any of those considered major.

The term "vaudeville" was coined by Benjamin Keith and Edward Albee, two of the giants in the field, to give their variety programs a more refined image than that of minstrel shows and the like. Their first vaudeville show was in Boston in 1885.

After the Trietsch Family Band days, Ken Trietsch reportedly played the tuba with both the Paul Whiteman and Vincent Lopez orchestras in New York. According to Brian Rust's extensive discographies of both dance and jazz band recordings, Ken was not a sideman on any records made by either Whiteman or Lopez. Neither cut a record before 1920, however, and it wasn't unusual for a band leader to recruit musicians other than those in his own band for recording sessions. Whether Whiteman or Lopez did it is not known, but in the teen years and early 'twenties some leaders had more than one set of musicians so bands under his name could appear at two or more locations at the same time.

No band came close to equaling Whiteman's in popularity during the 1920s. Many of his records even featured a cartoonish drawing of his head on the label. The drawings bore a striking resemblance to comedian Oliver Hardy.

Although billed as "The King of Jazz," Whiteman's band rarely played anything more than a carefully arranged version of jazz. This despite having many jazz greats in the band at various times including Bix Beiderbecke, Tommy and Jimmy Dorsey, Jack Teagarden, Bunny Berigan and numerous others. Jazz great Eddie Condon criticized Whiteman for "trying to make a lady out of jazz."

Playing for either Whiteman or Lopez would have greatly enhanced a musician's reputation, yet Ken seemed to quickly tire of life in the big city and was soon back in Cowan. There isn't much to be found there, but the Trietsch farm was close to the Union Traction interurban line linking Muncie and New Castle so the family would have had easy access to those larger cities and the world beyond.

A few miles due south of Cowan is another hamlet, Oakville. Not much there, either, aside from a grain elevator, but Oakville was once hit by a tornado or, as they were often called during that era, a cyclone. One of the early Hoosier Hot Shot recordings was "The Oakville Twister." It undoubtedly was written by Ken.

Was there something in the air around Cowan during the late 19th and early 20th centuries that bred singers and musicians? Before the Trietsch brothers there was Orville Harrold, a far different sort of entertainer who once sang in The Cowan Quartet. He had many credits to his name, chief among them being the lead tenor of the Metropolitan Opera Company following the death of Enrico Caruso.

When Harrold joined with Caruso and Rosa Ponselle in singing the opera La Juive, fellow operatic star Antonio Scotti said, "Never did I hear finer singing than in that trio."

HARROLD

A far cry from Buzzington's band or the Hoosier Hot Shots, yet Orville Harrold also enjoyed singing music lighter than operatic arias so he might have appreciated the boys had he not died just as they were getting started. His death, it was reported, came just after singing a

25

popular song of the early 1930s, "I'm Heading For The Last Roundup."

It would take a lengthy book to record the accomplishments of Orville Harrold. The ad below appeared in The Muncie Morning Star of May 7, 1911 when he returned to the area for a concert. At the time the Trietsch boys and Otto Ward were in elementary school.

WYSOR GRAND OPERA HOUSE
FRIDAY NIGHT ONLY, MAY 12

GREATEST OF AMERICAN TENORS

NO SEAT OVER $1.00

Seat Sale Opens Tomorrow---Lower Floor, 1.00;
3 Rows Balcony, 1.00; Balance Balcony,
75; Gallery, 50c

ORVILLE HARROLD

By Permission of Oscar Hammerstein

ADDITIONAL CONCERT

Musicians from Ft. Wayne,
Terre Haute, Etc.

SEATS MONDAY AT 9:00
50---75---1.00

All Included

The Hoosier Hot Shots appeared on the stage at the Wysor Grand during a Gala New Year's Eve Show in 1939. They also performed earlier in the day along with the movie "Henry Goes Arizona" starring Frank Morgan, Guy Kibbee and Slim Summerville. A few years later Kibbee and Summerville were in several movies with the boys. On the same program was a Lew Lehr short subject, Fox News and a travelogue on Peru – the country, not the town in Indiana. The cost for all this was 40 cents, a dime for kids.

Doors opened at 11:45 p.m. for the Gala New Year's Eve Show. Also on the program were Princess Adoree – the Turkish Dream Dancer, the local Goldcoasters Orchestra led by Carl "Doc" Noble and the movie "The Day the Bookies Wept" starring radio comedian Joe Penner and Betty Grable. All seats were 55 cents.

Betty Grable would become the favorite "pin-up girl" of GIs during World War II while Penner was known for his catch line, "Wanna buy a duck?" That and "Are you ready Hezzie?" were oft-quoted sayings at the time. That long ago night at the Wysor Grand in Muncie the audience would have heard both.

Orville Harrold's son, Paul, married my Aunt Ethel Lynch. This interested Evan Owens, who had the desk next to mine in the Muncie Evening Press newsroom. Evan was a pixyish little man with a dry Hoosier sense of humor. He was an exceptionally good writer who used his talent only in writing a twice-a-week column called *In the Press of Things*. Half a dozen years after his death I used that for the name of my daily column.

Evan had the knack of writing a paragraph or two on a subject, then going off on what appeared to be a complete tangent. Then in the final paragraph he would manage to tie it all together. This requires genuine skill, one I have attempted to emulate without ever quite coming up to Evan's standard.

Evan kept a row of Horatio Alger books against the wall at the rear of his desk and on quiet afternoons he would read one of them. One day I asked if they were good so he handed one to me and told me to read it. I did, and after that we would have lengthy conversations about these "boy makes good" stories, always seeming to be very serious but with our tongues firmly planted in cheek. A stranger listening would quickly have decided we had gone around the bend and were in desperate need of professional help. Perhaps that stranger would have been right.

Despite my efforts to assure him otherwise, Evan was convinced, or pretended to be, that my by-marriage tie to Orville Harrold meant I was blessed with an outstanding singing voice. Whenever the Evening Press had a party he would have a few drinks and then demand that I get up and sing. No amount of protesting on my part would convince him that singing was just one of many talents I failed to possess. He'd just sit there grinning and keep repeating, "Sing for us, Dick, sing for us." On a few occasions when I perhaps had taken one drink too many myself I would oblige. This resulted in hooting and catcalling and people sometimes throwing nickels and dimes in my direction.

There are those who say the Hoosier Hot Shots murdered music. I wholeheartedly disagree, but if by chance they happen to be right, I drove the final nail into the coffin.

I'm not certain just what it says about Munsonians – that's what residents of Muncie call themselves – but a great many of them could tell a visitor all about the Hoosier Hot Shots while very few are even a little familiar with Orville Harrold..

EZRA BUZZINGTON'S RUBE BAND

Most members of the Buzzington band were given nicknames fitting the image of Rustic Revelers. Otto Ward became Gabe Hawkins and Paul Trietsch was called Hezekiah. The latter was soon shortened to Hezzie and the name stuck, as did Gabe.

Ken Trietsch, handsome with combed back dark hair, bore a resemblance to the leading matinee idol of the era, Rudolph Valentino. Ken became Rudy Vaselino. He didn't much care for the moniker and when Valentino, the heartthrob of millions of female movie goers, suddenly died the name no longer was humorous. He reverted back to being Ken and the names of the three original Hot Shots had come into being – Hezzie, Gabe and Ken.

Mark Schaefer, the real name of Ezra Buzzington, formed his band in Eaton, Indiana, a small town ten miles or so north of Muncie on the road to Hartford City. Another small Hoosier village, Eaton boasted of a few stores, a Union Traction interurban station, some houses and not much more. The houses are still there in the 21st century but little else. For the sake of name recognition, Schaefer usually billed his band as being from Muncie, a fairly large city and much better known than Eaton. It was at Eaton, though, that the band rehearsed.

Hezzie married Bessie Burke of Darlington, Indiana in April of 1924 and for a while she was a member of the band. Ken also was married during his time with Buzzington. His wife, the former Ruth Maudlin of Daleville, wasn't a performer. Yet another Hoosier village, Daleville lies 14 miles southwest of Muncie and is best known as the place where John Dillinger pulled his first bank robbery.

Gabe was married, too, while with the band. That was in 1928. He had met Marguerite, his future bride, when the band had an engagement in Tiffin, Ohio, where she was attending college. Someone arranged for a couple of the girls to go out with two of the musicians and asked Marguerite which of them she wanted to date. "The one with the white teeth," she replied. One thing led to another and a wedding date was set. In a June 15, 1987 letter to me Gabe wrote:

"Marguerite 'n' I were to have been married in Toledo, Ohio on this day – June 15, 1928. The band was appearing at the old opera house in St. Louis, four shows a day, $850 per week. We were headlined. Played poker between shows, never took off our makeup all the time to go eat, etc.

"I was having a new H & M wardrobe trunk made at the St. Louis factory. It had an ironing board, jewel box, shoe box and special His and Hers drawers! Really tops for our trip to New York and Eastern vaudeville on Loew's Circuit.

"I lost so much in 5- and 10-cent poker that I set the wedding up to June 30th at Toledo. Stayed at the Secor Hotel on our wedding time and then to Napoleon, Ohio on the Maumee River for a four-day date. We packed 'em in and were held over two days. Made over $100 each (8 people) on percentage. The old clarinet duets with Hezzie's whistle were big stuff on 'Yearning' and 'Margie.'

"I wanted to buy a new clarinet. At the Pedler factory and others in Elkhart the average price was in the $90 range. But I was married now! Went to New York with the old horn 'n' new Marge. Folks said they liked a strong melody and I made a good sound. I guess I believed them and kept the old clarinet! I did buy a spare from a pawn shop for $35. Later I sold it to my Indianapolis cousin for $35. That was about 1938. I don't suppose he will ever pay me! Ha! Ha! He's a good ol' Hoosier."

Later Gabe wrote this:

"Marguerite never told me to quit the music biz. She was not a drop out (Gabe was), attended Tiffin Business College, and was a secretary in Toledo when we married. Her $20 per week salary sure helped out when Buzzington's band was not booked.

"Mark Schaefer – Ezra – had a farm at Farmland (Indiana) and could retreat to it and enjoy 'laying off.' We usually borrowed from him to get to the next engagement. He was a gentleman and a pal to us all! The band made $1200 per week in Keith-Albee's, Loew's, Orpheum and Pantages vaudeville circuits in 1923 to 1928. Was neat. We had a super novelty type, confused jazz. A bunch o' hicks. I have four sides we recorded at Starr Piano Co., Gennett label, Richmond, Indiana, 1925."

An Ezra Buzzington's Rube Band publicity photo taken in New Orleans during an engagement there on the Loew's vaudeville circuit in 1927. Gabe is standing at the left, Ken and Hezzie are in the rumble seat while on the running board are Tim Brown, banjo player from Anderson, Ind., Ezra and his wife Ola (Samantha), and standing is Art Sorenson, a trombone player from Eau Claire, Wis. The automobile is a new Jordan Sports Car. The Jordan was made in Cleveland and named for the company's founder, Edward S. "Ned" Jordan. He was a real promoter who revolutionized automobile advertising by getting away from dull copy citing specifications with his "Somewhere West of Laramie" ads featuring a speeding girl and a hatless cowboy. As a result the Jordan was considered a "man's man" car. Like so many other great automobiles, it failed to survive the devastating effects of the Great Depression. Ned Jordan saw it coming and unloaded most of his stock in the company in the late 1920s.

Somewhere West of Laramie

SOMEWHERE west of Laramie there's a broncho-
busting, steer-roping girl who knows what I'm
talking about.

She can tell what a sassy pony, that's a cross between
greased lightning and the place where it hits, can do with
eleven hundred pounds of steel and action when he's
going high, wide and handsome.

The truth is—the Playboy was built for her.

Built for the lass whose face is brown with the sun when
the day is done of revel and romp and race.

She loves the cross of the wild and the tame.

There's a savor of links about that car—of laughter and
lilt and light—a hint of old loves—and saddle and quirt.
It's a brawny thing—yet a graceful thing for the sweep
o' the Avenue.

Step into the Playboy when the hour grows dull with
things gone dead and stale.

Then start for the land of real living with the spirit of
the lass who rides, lean and rangy, into the red horizon
of a Wyoming twilight.

JORDAN

JORDAN MOTOR CAR COMPANY, Inc. Cleveland, Ohio

> **The ad that revolutionized automobile advertising. No more dull recitation of specifications after this one appeared.**

So the Buzzington band did well through the 1920s with some madcap antics and Hezzie playing the washboard he called his zither. Why he picked that name is a mystery because a legitimate stringed musical instrument called the zither is popular in many countries of Europe. It became known in America when Anton Karas used a zither to play the theme music for the classic film *The Third Man* starring Orson Welles and Joseph Cotton.

Gabe wrote this about the band's payroll: "Ken played a bass and because it was big and a hassle to travel with he got $15 per week more than the others. Ezra and wife Ola got $1,500 per week for the act. Paul on alto horn and slide whistle got $90 per week. Fred Ferg of Muncie on trombone got $75. I did all the leads on clarinet and sax and got $85."

That may not seem like much money, but it was. The average wage of the American worker was $750 per year. For farmers it was $273 a year. If Gabe worked a full 52 weeks he would have made $4,420. He didn't work that many weeks, of course.

Gabe continued, "I had earned the title of public relations man. For no special reason I always did many interviews with reporters and radio people and loved the intrigue of meeting special folks at special events. I vowed to go into some phase of public relations if I lost fingers and couldn't do the old licorice stick.

"Many of the band's odd instruments were made by the five Trietsch brothers, who lived on a farm out of Muncie. Joe was a pattern maker at General Motors in Pontiac, Mich. and fashioned wood into saxophones, trumpet, slide trombone, etc."

Vaudeville took a hit, though, when silent movies gave way to the talkies in the late 'twenties and at the same time more and more Americans were getting their entertainment from radio, the new-fangled device that brought it right into their homes. Then in October of 1929 Wall Street took its notorious nosedive and the Great Depression was underway. If talking pictures and radio had dealt vaudeville a painful blow, the Depression made it fatal.

Mark Schaefer realized the end was near and broke up the band in 1929 when Gabe, Ken and Hezzie quit. He continued on in show business, eventually leading the studio band for the Lum 'n' Abner radio show. This was a tremendously popular program for more than twenty years and tapes of it are still sold today. Two men, Chester Lauck and Norris Goff, did all of the many voices and made the Jot 'em Down store in Pine Ridge, Arkansas familiar to millions of listeners. The program was so popular that the little town of Waters, which served as its model, changed its name to Pine Ridge.

In many ways the careers of Lauck and Goff paralleled those of Hezzie, Ken and Gabe. They, too, were heard on radio at the time the Hoosier Hot Shots were broadcasting. They went to Hollywood in 1939 and made seven Lum 'n' Abner movies during the next decade and their sponsor for much of that time was Alka-Seltzer, just as it was for the Hot Shots.

After the break-up of the Buzzington band, Ken, Gabe and Hezzie found jobs at Montgomery Ward stores in Lima and Van Wert, Ohio, but also were making music together whenever possible. Art Sorenson dropped out of sight and Tim Brown came down with TB and died an early death.

The band's name lived on, though, when Schaefer's grandson, Jonathan Harris, an actor, director and writer, chose Ezra Buzzington as his professional name.

GABE WARD WROTE THE NOTES ON THIS
VAUDEVILLE PROGRAM FROM SEATTLE

34

RECORDING AT GENNETT

A recording session at the Gennett studio in Richmond, Indiana highlighted 1925 for Ezra Buzzington's Rube Band. There doesn't seem to be an accurate account of how many sides were cut but Gabe Ward sent five of them to me on tape. An odd number would be unusual for obvious reasons although it wasn't totally unheard of in those days.

The Gennett story is fascinating in itself. The last place in the world you would expect to find a record company would be a medium-size town in Indiana, but there was a good reason for it. Gennett was a subsidiary of the Starr Piano Company and it was located in Richmond.

It began in the 19th century when Starr hired Henry Gennett as secretary-treasurer. He was a man of many ideas and one of them was to get in on the booming business of making phonograph records. In 1916 a six story brick building for that purpose was constructed on the 23-acre Starr complex on low ground along South 1st Street. The property was beside the Whitewater River, a source of water power. That was fine for building pianos and the other merchandise turned out at the sprawling complex.

However, for recording 78 r.p.m. phonograph records there was a problem. A railroad track followed the path of the river so it passed close beside the Starr buildings. During the day traffic on the line was heavy at times and the sound of a freight train rumbling by did not make for good background accompaniment on a record.

There wasn't any choice other than to cut records when everything was quiet. That sometimes meant pausing and starting over again. That could be a nuisance, but Gennett's routine eased the problem. Unlike the giants in the industry, Victor and Columbia, who sometimes recorded a dozen or more takes, Gennett settled for spontaneity. This was just fine because the majority of its early records featured jazz groups and orchestras that for the most part were shunned by the big companies. When recording jazz, one or two takes was best. It worked fine, too, with country singers and groups.

A list of the artists who recorded at Gennett reads like a roster of jazz greats with a few country singers and an occasional conventional band thrown in. In 2007 the Starr-Gennett Foundation in Richmond began a Walk of Fame near the site of the old studio. The first ten honored were Louis Armstrong, Bix Beiderbecke, Jelly Roll Morton, Joe "King" Oliver, Hoagy Carmichael, Big Bill Broonzy, Georgia Tom, Gene Autry, Vernon Dalhart and Lawrence Welk.

Yes, Lawrence Welk. Not jazz, not country, but basically a polka band at the time he recorded for Gennett. The second group to be inducted includes Guy Lombardo, proving that bands and artists as conventional as you can get also recorded for Gennett. Others in the second group are Fats Waller, Duke Ellington, Coleman Hawkins, Blind Lemon Jefferson, Fletcher Henderson, Sidney Bechet, Charley Patton, Homer Rodeheaver and Uncle Dave Macon. Many more musical legends recorded for Gennett.

Gennett didn't do all its recording in Richmond. In the beginning it was done at a studio in New York until the new one in Richmond was finished in 1921. The pressing was done either in Richmond or Montreal. At times Gennett recorded in Chicago. In 1927, Southern blues and jazz were recorded at the Starr Piano store in Birmingham. At St. Paul, Minnesota records were made of German, Polish and Swedish folk music.

In 1926 Gennett, like other companies, switched from the old acoustic system to electrical recording and began issuing discs with "Electrobeam" added to the label. The new, improved system was not the reason sales began falling that year. A major factor was the rapidly increasing popularity of radio, but there were others as well.

Perhaps anticipating the coming changes, in 1925 Gennett began issuing records under the Champion label to supply chain stores with bargain-priced records. It soon went a step further by reissuing old Gennett masters with a red Champion label, frequently not identifying the artists by their real names to prevent having to pay them royalties. Whether the company was ever challenged on this deceptive practice isn't known.

Gennett also issued records under such labels as Black Patti (for "race" records), Challenge, Conqueror, Bell, Buddy, Silvertone (for Sears-Roebuck), Superior and Supertone.

With the Great Depression drastically reducing the sales of records – and everything else – Gennett ceased production under its own name late in 1930 but continued releasing them under bargain-priced labels. Champion managed to hang on until late 1934. The new, aggressive and well-financed Decca then bought much of Gennett's material and rights.

So, like so many other once-thriving businesses, Gennett fell victim to the Great Depression although it did continue issuing sound effect recordings for movies and radio. Starr went on making pianos until 1949, then it too faded away.

In 1981 the vacant Starr-Gennett buildings were leveled. Those who managed to pick up some of the bricks were able to sell them to jazz collectors for a hefty price. The same is true for those possessing many of the old Gennett records.

Henry Gennett, the man responsible for Starr Piano going into the record business, rose to be president of the company and remained in that position until his death in 1922. All three of his sons were employed by the firm. When the Victor Talking Machine Co. filed a patent infringement suit against the Starr Piano Co. in 1922, a Circuit Court of Appeals ruled against Victor.

HENRY GENNETT

It isn't likely that the members of Ezra Buzzington's Rube Band knew any of that. It's less likely that they would have cared. So what songs did they really record that day in 1925? The Hoosier Hot Shots Museum website lists four and you can hear all of them there. The titles are *Bass Blues, Brown Jug Blues, Down Among The Sugar Cane,* and *Rollin' Home*. A fifth, *Alfalfa*, was sent to me on tape by Gabe. In his outstanding book "American Premium Record Guide 1900-1965," Les Docks lists both *Alfalfa* and the elusive sixth, *Kansas City Kitty*. It was a hit song by pop recording artists of that era including Rudy Vallee. Docks doesn't list *Down Among The Sugar Cane* or *Rollin' Home*. He prices all Buzzington records from $100 to $250 on the open market or at auction.

Alfalfa might best be described as an upbeat jazz tune with Ken coming in heavy on the tuba – really dominating all else.

Gabe, speaking on the tape after the music, listed the following sidemen on the Gennett recordings: Ken Trietsch on tuba, Hezzie Trietsch on cymbals, Gabe Ward on clarinet, Frank Kettering on piccolo and Mark Schaefer (Ezra) doing most of the singing. There were more sidemen on the recordings but Gabe spoke only of Ezra and future Hoosier Hot Shots.

38

THE GREAT DEPRESSION BRINGS BOTH MISERY AND OPPORTUNITY

The era of vaudeville – and the Buzzington Band – ended with a thud in 1929 and another much darker one began, The Great Depression. To put the rise of the Hoosier Hot Shots into perspective it is necessary to have at least a rudimentary knowledge of those bleak years and what it was that brought them about.

Americans who didn't live through it may find it difficult to imagine how really horrible conditions were from the last two months of 1929 until early spring of 1933. The Depression dragged on for many more years after 1933, of course, but it had bottomed out and from the day Franklin D. Roosevelt became president hope for the future was revived.

In his book *The Great Depression,* Robert S. McElvaine shows that its roots lay in the 1920s. Values and attitudes changed during the years after the First World War as people became more self-centered and placed greater importance on financial gain. Americans wanted not only everything that was new, they wanted the newest of the new. In order to have it they willingly spent more money than they earned. Going into debt was encouraged by merchants offering easy credit so "enjoy now and pay later" became a way of life for Americans. That the bill would eventually fall due seemed of little concern to people. Far more appealing was the perceived need for instant gratification, the belief that a happy and fulfilled life was impossible without possessing all the marvelous and new products flooding the marketplace..

In the decade beginning in 1919 the number of automobiles in the United States increased from 7 to 23 million. People began thinking of the family car as a necessity, not a luxury available only to people financially independent. In his 1928 presidential campaign, Herbert Hoover promised, "A chicken in every pot, two cars in every garage." Not too much time would pass before people were repeating wry, bitter jokes about not even having a pot.

The coming of commercial radio brought new methods of advertising encouraging listeners to spend, spend, spend. Newspapers and magazines joined the chorus until it seemed that frugality was almost un-American. Forgotten by most was the old way of looking at life and its message warning young people to, "Lay your pennies by the rocks and you'll always have tobacco in your old tobacco box." Who needed a tobacco box when cigarette manufacturers sang the constant refrain that comfort and satisfaction were available for a quarter per pack at every grocery and drug store in the land?

Then there was the new and easy path to riches – the stock market. Once the province of men of substance, it now provided the road to the good life for members of the middle class, common folks who worked for a living. Investing whatever you could, including your life savings, was the smart thing to do, or so people came to believe. After all, it just kept going up, up, up and no one could imagine that it might come crashing down and leave them penniless.

So there it was, a giant bubble involving the vast majority of Americans. Millions were driving shiny new cars, living in comfortable homes complete with the latest furnishings and appliances and all the while forgetting their fine possessions really belonged to the banks and finance companies so they actually owned nothing at all. Completing the picture was the stack of beautiful, engraved stock certificates guaranteeing a happy, secure future. Why give even a thought to the fact they were purchased on margin and actually were nothing more than pieces of paper?

As the years went by the Roaring Twenties truly revolutionized the way Americans both lived and thought. Prohibition was a nuisance, of course, but speakeasies sprouted up everywhere so people who had never been inside a tavern and otherwise might have remained teetotalers found it exciting to knock on a door and say, "Joe sent me," to the man peering at them through a peephole. Men of means boasted of having their own bootlegger who could supply the real thing brought in from Canada, or at least a reasonable facsimile.

The liquor indeed flowed freely and no one with a thirst had trouble finding it. Some of it was rotgut and some of it –

gin – was concocted in bathtubs, but who really cared? Not the patrons of the speakeasies. Certainly not the wealthy because they had a steady supply of the real thing: Scotch, Canadian, Irish and rye whiskey smuggled in from Canada or even Europe. Not the workingman who knew where to find a cold glass of beer after a hard day in the factory, mill or mine.

While Prohibition didn't stop people from drinking it did bring gang territorial wars to major cities, chief among them Chicago, New York and Detroit. Al Capone became a household name throughout the country and just as familiar to people in Chicago was that of his chief rival, Dion O'Banion. When O'Banion was gunned down in the florist shop where he nurtured the flowers he dearly loved, the names of his successors, Hymie Weiss and Bugs Moran, soon were just as well known. New York's Frankie Yale and Dutch Schultz along with the Purple Gang in Detroit gained nationwide notoriety.

Americans fascinated by the escapades of the leading gangsters didn't realize the advent of Prohibition with its opportunity for seemingly easy money and illegal activity also firmed up something in its infancy – organized crime. Weak at the beginning, it seized on Prohibition to quickly grow strong and soon its tentacles reached to every sizable city in the country. Once established, it wouldn't go away without a fight.

Gangsters in Chicago were particularly active in killing each other and many an innocent bystander was caught in the crossfire. Corrupt politicians and law enforcement officials were on the payrolls of various gangs and stories of chicanery involving men in positions of authority became commonplace. The Teapot Dome Scandal during the administration of Warren G. Harding created widespread cynicism and accustomed Americans to corruption in high places.

Everything was in a state of flux. Silent movies gave way to the talkies, radios were found in an ever increasing number of homes, nearly everyone had a phonograph, the record business flourished and the polite, staid music played by society orchestras gave way to jazz and upbeat bands supplied with an endless number of new tunes by Tin Pan Alley. The sedate waltz was replaced by the wild gyrations of the fox trot, the Charleston and the Black Bottom.

The Paul Whiteman band led all others in popularity. The Revelers featuring future Metropolitan Opera singer James Melton was the leading vocal group, Ruth Etting was tops among the torch singers and Gene Austin's falsetto singing set the standard for male vocalists.

Old taboos against women smoking cigarettes or drinking alcoholic beverages were forgotten in the Roaring Twenties. Young females who a decade earlier would have believed that displaying an ankle was risqué now were wearing flimsy short skirts and rolled-down stockings. Many saw no need for undergarments even when climbing up a fender to enter a car's rumble seat. The automobiles that had become so commonplace provided bedrooms on wheels. After looking at young women, the flappers of the 1920s, historian Paul Fass said, ". . . the traditionalist saw the end of American civilization as he had known it."

Lindbergh flew across the Atlantic and suddenly the airplane was seen as something more than a novelty or an activity for daring young men flying Sopwith Camels and Fokker D-7s in mortal combat. Every city of any size had an airport, in some places several of them, and the major ports grew steadily bigger to accommodate airplanes that also were growing increasingly larger. Fledgling airlines began operation and it wasn't long before scheduled flights between major cities became accepted as a new form of transportation. Ford

Tri-Motor transport planes would become a familiar site until newer, sleeker models from Douglas and Boeing replaced them in the 1930s. Numerous companies were building private planes from early in the decade, making the Roaring Twenties even louder.

Airmail service began between certain cities but many of the early flights ended in disaster. Of the first fifty pilots to make the New York to Chicago run, forty-one were killed in crashes.

Huge dirigibles attracted crowds wherever they passed overhead and much smaller blimps were rapidly multiplying. The U.S. Navy pioneered the dirigible in this country. The nation was shocked when in 1925 the giant Navy airship Shenandoah broke in two and crashed during a storm in Southern Ohio. Despite that setback, plans went ahead to build two even larger dirigibles at a giant hanger in Akron.

The Black Sox scandal was forgotten as Babe Ruth, Lou Gehrig and other muscular athletes hit more and more homeruns. Red Grange was a national hero and the nation was fascinated by the Four Horsemen of Notre Dame. An interesting pastime for some in earlier years, college football became big business during the decade.

Even as far back as the 1920s Americans were fascinated by celebrities and the sensational. At various times the entire nation was captivated by such diverse events as the Scopes "monkey" trial in Tennessee, the search for a young man named Floyd Collins who had disappeared in a Kentucky cave, the execution of alleged anarchists Sacco and Vanzetti, and the brutal "just for a lark" murder of youthful Bobby Franks by Nathan Leopold and Richard Loeb, both post-graduate college students and the sons of well-to-do parents. Famed defense attorney Clarence Darrow saved Leopold and Loeb from the death penalty and in the Scopes trial made a fool of William Jennings Bryan.

F. Scott Fitzgerald was the darling of the literary world and writers such as Ernest Hemingway and Dashiell Hammett were writing down-to-earth stories about real life in a terse, sparse style unknown in the past. The world revolved around youth with a capital Y.

Conservatives managed to bring about large decreases in taxes for the wealthy as well as for corporations. Many of them believed they should pay no taxes at all and the entire burden should fall upon the working class. Some pushed for the repeal of Prohibition so a tax could be placed on beer, the workingman's drink. Others tried to gain control of the Democratic Party so that the wealthy would be in charge of the entire political process. Herbert Hoover, an arch conservative himself, said, "The only trouble with capitalism is capitalists. They're too damned greedy."

Then with little or no warning the bubble burst and it all came crashing down. Even most insiders were taken by surprise by that October 1929 debacle. *Variety*, the bible of the entertainment business, came up with the best headline. From that point onward there proved to be little humor in the news.

The unemployment rate quickly shot up to 24.9 per cent and even those who had a job were in constant fear that their own turn might come next. The blow hit the working class the hardest but even doctors and lawyers could be found out on the street. Middle class people who had invested in the stock market lost everything. Houses, furniture and cars were repossessed. Soon numerous banks began to fail so even those who had prudently saved their money saw it disappear.

Hoovervilles, shantytowns of tents and shelters constructed of wood and cardboard, sprang up in every city of any size. They were named for Hoover, the president foolish enough to heed the advice of archconservatives who told him to "ride it out." Among them was multi-millionaire Andrew Mellon,

44

Secretary of the Treasury. His advice was, "Liquidate labor, liquidate stocks, liquidate the farmers, liquidate real estate." One can only wonder what he believed would be left.

To avoid having people starving to death on the streets, breadlines opened up throughout the country. Men desperate for a job hit the road in search of work and some became the hoboes or bums that traveled wherever railroads could take them. A number of humorous "bum" songs were recorded. One great line came when a hobo knocked on a door and said to the housewife who answered, "Mum, I've got a button here. Would you mind sewing a shirt on it?"

Thousands of men were selling apples on street corners and *Brother, Can You Spare a Dime?* became hit songs for both Bing Crosby and Rudy Vallee. Men uttering that plea were found on every city street. Billy Durant, founder of General Motors and a car company bearing his own name, was reduced to working as a short-order cook in a bowling alley.

Never able to descend from his ivory tower, never able to comprehend how terrible conditions really were for millions of Americans, Herbert Hoover later wrote in his memoir that during the early 1930s, "Many persons left their jobs for the more profitable one of selling apples."

Forgetting that millions of men were out of work and that those with jobs were fearful of losing them even though their wages were low, Hoover said the depression would end if people just started spending money. That led to a popular tongue-in-cheek song that included the line, "Mr. Herbert Hoover says now's the time to buy, so let's have another cup of coffee, and let's have another piece of pie."

A hit song was *Boulevard of Broken Dreams* and another became known as The Suicide Song because so many people killed themselves after hearing *Gloomy Sunday*. Numerous radio stations banned it because of the outbreak of deaths.

Not too many people were singing, however, during those first few years of the Great Depression. Although only four at the time of the crash, this writer saw his traveling salesman father lose his job, then his mother lose hers as nurse at the Fox Theatre in Detroit. One by one all their possessions were lost. Clyde Stodghill did manage to come up with an old and decrepit Model-T Ford touring car. It had a canvas top but was open on both sides. After traveling from town to town looking for work and finding none, for a time the Model-T became the only home the family knew.

So in brief that was the situation when Gabe, Ken and Hezzie found themselves in need of jobs. So did millions of other men but that wouldn't have discouraged the boys one bit. If their characteristics had been listed either at the time or in the future, lack of confidence would not have been among them. They not only found jobs, they held onto them. It was music, though, that was their real interest so whenever they had a little spare time they practiced the songs and routines that soon would help bring a little cheer to a country in desperate need of it.

BIRTH OF THE HOOSIER HOT SHOTS

No matter how they looked at it, selling washing machines and other merchandise for Montgomery Ward at two locations in Western Ohio couldn't have been much fun. It was a big comedown after having spent years touring the country on the vaudeville circuits, playing the music they loved, clowning around on the stage and just having a good time in general.

The one positive factor was that it allowed them to meet people. A smile, a handshake, some cheerful talk at a time when there wasn't much to be cheerful about. At that Gabe, Ken and Hezzie had few peers. Perhaps that was what enabled them to hold onto jobs when so many people were losing them. Not the kind of jobs they really wanted, of course, but at least something to put food on the table. All were married now and no longer footloose young fellows without responsibilities other than to themselves.

Washing machines were a relatively new product helping ease the Monday morning workload for women fortunate enough to own one. Using a washing machine still required considerable work but nothing like the backbreaking, knuckle-scraping job of scrubbing clothes on a washboard. After the machine did the washing, clothes had to be rinsed, run through the wringer that was attached to the machine, put in a basket and hung up to dry. That was accomplished on outdoor clotheslines except on rainy or frigid days. Then they were dried on lines in the basement, something that added considerable humidity to the house. It also meant working your way around them when it was time to throw a little more coal in the furnace.

Women of the 21st century, accustomed to automatic washers and driers, would find using one of those old washing machines a terrible imposition. At the time, however, they were considered a wonderful time saver, a welcome relief from the worst feature of wash day. Some women swore they didn't do the job as thoroughly as the old method but they were soon won over, especially by an outgoing young salesman.

Despite their need to spend their days working at mundane jobs the boys managed to get together in the evenings and on days off to play a little music. Many a time they drove sixty-five miles or more each way to practice or play at an event with the Muncie Products Band. The firm, a subsidiary of General Motors, manufactured auto parts at a plant on East Eighth Street. Working there wasn't a requirement for playing in the band, especially for those with extraordinary talent.

That really wasn't their kind of music even though it was better than no music at all, so they soon worked up a routine and a repertoire of their own. Some of it carried over from their Buzzington days, some consisted of contemporary tunes, some of it original compositions. Ken was responsible for most of the latter but Gabe did his part too. There was a touch of jazz, a little ragtime and Dixieland and some cornball jokes told in a way that even sophisticates could find amusing. But when the mood struck, the boys could play more conventional, even beautiful, music. But their stock in trade was fun. Or, as Gabe later put it, "stupid." They billed themselves as the Trietsch Brothers and Ward, an insipid, uninspiring name for three young men who normally were quick on the trigger with impromptu ideas and acts.

It very likely was Ken who managed to convince the management at WOWO, a powerful Fort Wayne radio station heard in much of Northern Indiana, Southern Michigan and Western Ohio, that giving the Trietsch Brothers and Ward their own fifteen minute show would both please and enhance the listening audience. Of the many breaks that came their way over the years, that was one of the biggest. They weren't paid for their efforts, but the idea was to gain bookings in the surrounding area and the radio show certainly accomplished that.

It wasn't long before they began earning a few bucks playing at clubs and social affairs in and around Fort Wayne. Little towns such as Auburn, Decatur and Van Wert, Ohio just across the state line were fertile ground for their jolly, down-home routines. Their first booking was at the Elks Club in Van Wert. They were paid $15 for their performance and most of those that followed, not bad money at the time.

According to a story believed by many, an announcer at WOWO gave the boys a big boost. They were running late one day and the announcer was in a tizzy. If they failed to show up, how was he going to fill that fifteen minutes of air time? With the fateful moment at hand he heard Hezzie, Gabe and Ken milling around outside the studio. He opened the door and heatedly cried, "Hey, you Hoosier hot shots, get in here!"

You can almost picture the scene: the boys hurriedly starting their act and the relieved announcer wiping his brow. Later, as they were leaving, Hezzie saying something funny and Gabe giving him a light poke on the arm while saying, "You Hoosier hot shot." And then the dawning of the light, the sudden realization that here was a great name for the act, The Hoosier Hot Shots. Memorable, descriptive of their happy-go-lucky style of music. Far better than the dry, forgettable Trietsch Brothers and Ward. It's a great tale, but is it true?

Not according to Gabe. The cutlines below tell a different story in his own words. .The somewhat blurry lines read: BELOVED TRIO . . . Gabe Ward wrote to Stodghill: "Dick,

BELOVED TRIO . . . Gabe Ward wrote to Stodghill: "Dick, this was our first photo of Trietsch Brothers and Ward, 'The Three Hot Shots.' WLS Radio named us 'The Hoosier Hot Shots' during the 1933 World's Fair and sold us to the 'Big Yank' shirt n' overall manufacturer — Wow!" From left are Ken, Hezzie and Gabe.

this was our first photo of Trietsch Brothers and Ward. 'The Three Hot Shots.' WLS Radio named us 'The Hoosier Hot Shots' during the 1933 World's Fair and sold us to the 'Big Yank' shirt and overall manufacturer – Wow!" From left are Ken, Hezzie and Gabe.

The photo accompanied a story I wrote for my employer, the Muncie Evening Press. So the naming of the Hoosier Hot Shots wasn't a chance happening. Before going to Chicago the Trietsch Brothers and Ward were referring to themselves as "The Three Hot Shots." Officials at WLS in Chicago dropped "Three" and added "Hoosier." Doing so made sense.

To enhance their disreputable look for the picture, Hezzie blackened a tooth to make it appear missing. And that hat . . .! Ken and Gabe went to great lengths to make themselves appear to be a pair of hicks attempting to look fashionable. They succeeded admirably.

The boys never tried to make good the easy way. They did it one group at a time, even one person at a time. If there was a gathering of any kind, a county fair, a carnival or just about anything else, Ken, Hezzie and Gabe were there. Even when they weren't on the program they'd show up, talk to people, shake hands, kid around a little and manage to make themselves known. It wasn't because a public relations person told them to do it, nor was it a contrived way of drumming up a following. No, it was just the way they were. They were doing what they wanted to do, have a good time and in the process make friends and help others enjoy themselves.

Saying they sang, joked and laughed their way through the Great Depression would be the truth. But it wasn't easy, making people smile during those grim years. They were in the heart of automobile country, towns and cities where cars were manufactured or people worked at turning out the parts that made them run. Indianapolis, Anderson, Muncie, Marion, Kokomo – those and a number of other towns relied on the automotive industry.

One by one many of the great names in the business went under – Stutz, Marmon, Reo, Hupmobile, Jordan, Peerless, Auburn, the Frankin air-cooled, and many others. They received no help from the government and certainly not from the Big Three – General Motors, Ford and Chrysler. A few consolidated and hung on for a while by doing so. In South Bend, Studebaker managed to survive the Depression and World War II, but not too many years after that it also vanished from the scene. The same was true of Packard and Hudson.

It was in the little town of Auburn not far north of Fort Wayne that the cars bearing that name were made. They were fine cars and most models sold at a reasonable price. Some said that was why the company failed to survive. Their cars were priced a little too high for the average man but too low for the affluent who mistakenly equated price with value. The most famous of the Auburns were the boat-tail speedsters. Every one was test driven at more than a hundred miles an hour.

A 1932 AUBURN SEDAN

The firm had another plant not far to the south in Connersville. Auburn also built the Cord, a beautiful car named for the company's president, E.L. Cord. Its coffin-nosed models turned heads wherever they were driven and are prized by collectors. It was another company product, however, that set the standard for elegance, the Duesenberg. So highly

51

regarded were they that a popular expression of the era, "It's a Doozie," meant something was the very best. The time would come when owning one could cost a collector hundreds of thousands of dollars.

So that was home country for the Hoosier Hot Shots. Gabe said they made their first record in 1932 and sent a copy of it to me on tape. Unfortunately it didn't arouse my curiosity at the time. I should have asked where it was cut and whether it was released to the public or was just a promo disc for their own use. It was one of those things you pass over lightly at the time, then later when it's too late wish you had pursued.

Chances are it was made at the Starr Piano Company in Richmond. The firm had quit producing records with the Gennett label but was still turning out a few for other companies and groups or individuals who desired one of their own. The boys had recorded six sides there in 1925 with the Buzzington band so they were familiar with the setup.

On the first side recorded, *The Cheer Parade,* Ken asked the question that would become so familiar: "Are you ready, Hezzie?" Aside from Ken still playing the tuba, the sound was typical of the group, although not as smooth and refined as later recordings. Ken's tuba somewhat dominated the flip side, *Virginia Blues.* A few years later they again recorded *Virginia Blues* and a later version of *The Cheer Parade* was one of many songs included on an electrical transcription.

Right from the start the Hoosier Hot Shots gave Americans something they badly needed in those dark days – a reason to smile, perhaps even laugh aloud. Long years later Gabe summed it up this way: "All we wanted to do was cheer up the 1929 Crash victims. It worked!"

Perhaps it was intentional or perhaps it wasn't, but an endearing part of their routine was looking the part of guys off the street who didn't realize they were sometimes making fools of themselves. Much like today's karaoke. Rarely did they dress up in corny outfits with pieces of straw sticking out of their mouths and hair. When they did it usually was the idea of a publicity man who didn't really get it. The vast majority of the time they wore street clothes: suits, neckties, and hats that fell just a shade short of being in style. You might say they looked the part of three or four guys who got up to perform while completely unaware of their lack of talent. It took great talent to put that over, and they did it. They could be funny because it usually didn't seem that they were trying to be funny. That might be because they didn't have to try, it just came naturally.

THE ORIGINAL HOT SHOTS – HEZZIE, GABE, KEN

None of that applied when they were performing in front of a camera in Hollywood, of course. That was another world, a world far removed from their roots on the flatlands of Central Indiana. In many ways the three core Hot Shots were an enhanced version of the people found in that part of the country. A dry sense of humor, a heightened awareness of the ironic, a disdain for those who put on airs, all of these are common characteristics of Hoosiers.

To many of them a creek is a crick, a fish is a feesh, a bush is a boosh and the machines Gabe sold at Montgomery Ward were used for warshing clothes. Sometimes syllables that seem a bit superfluous are dropped. Many would tell you that a good place to go feeshing is along the Missinewa rather than the Mississinewa River. A few might say the state capital is Indanapolis because calling it Indianapolis involves some unnecessary tongue wagging.

For some reason a number of Central Indiana towns bear the names of South American countries, but you don't pronounce them quite the same. There is BRAY-zil and PEE-rue and Chy-Lie. Elsewhere they might call the latter Chili. Down a little piece to the south is Loogootee. Now no self respecting Hoosier would be caught dead saying Loo-goo-tee so it comes out Luh-go-tee, or something like that.

Then there's the old Hoosier joke that says, "Indiana is a mixed up place because South Bend is in the north, North Vernon is in the south and we won't even talk about French Lick."

The late comedian Herb Shriner built a career around Hoosierisms. He often said, "I wasn't born in Indiana but I came as soon as I heard about it."

And Walter Winchell, don't even mention the old radio news reporter to some elderly Hoosiers. He reportedly said, although no one actually heard him say it, they just heard about him saying it from someone else, "Wise men come from Indiana. The wiser they are the sooner they come."

So that's just the way it is in the land where Hezzie, Ken and Gabe first saw the light of day and spent their formative years. Take it or leave it, most Hoosiers wouldn't care. "If you don't like it here, just go somewhere else," they'd tell you.

One of the first assignments I had after going to work for the Muncie Evening Press was covering a meeting in which a national dignitary from one of the service clubs – Lions, Rotary, I don't remember which – came to town to set the local members straight on something they weren't doing according to form. He talked for twenty or thirty minutes and everyone smiled and nodded their heads at everything he had to say. When he finally finished, and I had begun to wonder if he ever would, everyone applauded and went on nodding their heads. Then the local president stood up, still smiling, walked over and shook the speaker's hand and said, "Now let me tell you how we do it in Muncie."

That's Muncie. That's Indiana. You can talk until you're blue in the face and unless you have a clearly better way of doing something you won't get Hoosiers to change their ways. Take it or leave it, that's just the way it is.

If I've neglected to mention it before, I was born in Muncie – Middletown U.S.A. The city earned that title at the time Gabe, Ken and Hezzie were touring the country with the Ezra Buzzington band. A pair of sociologists, Robert S. and Helen Lynd, conducted a detailed study of the people in the city, which they called Middletown. Everyone immediately recognized it as Muncie despite the fact that only a few miles to the south in Henry County there is a genuine Middletown.

The study by the Lynds is still used in many college classrooms, as is their follow-up a dozen years later, "Middletown In Transition." It might be a safe bet that not more than a dozen residents of Muncie ever have or ever will read "Middletown" from cover to cover. It hardly qualifies as a page-turner. At the time it was published, however, many people did read the juicy parts. Some laughed when they thought they recognized someone pictured as a pompous idiot. Others grew indignant, believing they were the person thusly portrayed. Chief among those outraged was my grandfather, J.T. Lynch, manager of Metropolitan Life Insurance Company's Muncie office. While J.T. wasn't an idiot, he was pompous to the core.

Although they were young men at the time, much could be learned about the makeup of Ken, Gabe and Hezzie by reading "Middletown." The Lynds went astray in analyzing many aspects of Muncie, but they did accurately size up Hoosier characteristics.

So as 1932, very likely the worst year in American history, finally drew to a close the Hoosier Hot Shots were about to start down the road leading to nationwide recognition.

Franklin D. Roosevelt moved into the White House and programs to help Americans cope with the unimaginable difficulties were quickly put in place. Those difficulties were never fully appreciated by Herbert Hoover and his associates. Improvement didn't take place overnight, but now Americans saw light in the distance and were ready to smile again, even laugh aloud. With the help of radio it was provided to them by those three boys from Indiana, Hezzie, Gabe and Ken – the Hoosier Hot Shots.

WLS – THE PATH TO FAME

The popularity of their show on WOWO led to an opportunity the Hoosier Hot Shots had hoped for, one that would change their lives forever. It came when they were offered a chance to appear on The National Barn Dance, a tremendously popular program broadcast every Saturday night on radio station WLS in Chicago and heard nationwide on the NBC Blue Network.

The WLS story began nearly a decade earlier at the time when commercial radio was in its infancy. Bulky and cumbersome radio receivers were difficult to tune, required large storage batteries for operation and stations were few and far between. That didn't deter entertainment-hungry Americans, always on the lookout for the latest in gadgets and technology, from gobbling them up. Some people claimed it was a passing fancy destined to go the way of hoop skirts and the horse and buggy. Other wiser, more far sighted men saw radio for what it was: the wave of the future with limitless opportunity for making money.

Executives at Sears Roebuck were among the latter. For many years the company had been *the* place for farm families to shop for their every need aside from food. The majority had never actually seen a Sears store but did their buying from the company's popular catalog. City dwellers *could* visit a Sears store and many did even though they had numerous others to choose from. However, despite a network of interurban railways serving rural areas and the ever-increasing popularity of the automobile, farmers were isolated and relied upon the dependable catalog for their needs. There was little a family could possibly want that wasn't found somewhere in the huge book printed on cheap pulp paper. Profusely illustrated, it was updated yearly.

The arrival of a new issue was cause for rejoicing. Thousands of farmers and their wives spent long winter evenings poring over its pages, the men checking out the latest in farm equipment and accessories, the women admiring the current fashions in clothing or looking over the labor saving devices that seemed to multiply in number every year.

The old, outdated catalog was banished to the outhouse, where its pages served a useful purpose. In a recording describing how to construct the little building out back, Chic Sales noted that a family would never need to buy paper for it "as long as Sears Roebuck keeps a goin'." With normal usage, he said, "You should reach the harness section 'long about the first of May."

All that seemed threatened by the advent of radio, at least in the minds of the leading executives at Sears Roebuck. They experimented with radio commercials but weren't too happy with the results. What was needed, they concluded, was their own station with broadcasts aimed at the farm audience. In short order Sears acquired the rights to set up a 500 watt station, then built a transmitter and a studio. After several test broadcasts the station was ready for its formal debut on April 12, 1924. The call letters selected, WLS, stood for World's Largest Store. At the time, Sears Roebuck was entitled to make that claim.

Big plans were made for the evening of the initial broadcast. Sears officials and numerous other dignitaries attended a banquet at the WLS studio in the posh Sherman House Hotel and actress Ethyl Barrymore, a key member of the nation's leading theatrical family, was hired to say the first words when the station went on the air at 6 p.m. Things went a bit awry when Barrymore entered the studio and was taken aback by the size of the brand new microphone. Unaware that her words would be heard by everyone tuned in for the big moment, she cried, "Turn that damned thing off!"

And thus was WLS launched, although not quite as formally as planned. "It was a grand opening," said program director Edgar Bill, "never to be forgotten by those in attendance." Or, he might have added, by the listeners tuned in to hear Ethyl Barrymore's introductory words.

Sears didn't miss a bet in selling radio related merchandise to the public. Not only did they sell radio receivers, they also marketed such accessories and key components as external speakers and vacuum tubes bearing either the company name or Silvertone, a brand name that would continue in use down through the years.

One of the offbeat features of the station's early days was the use of a parrot called Static to assist George D. Hay, the chief announcer at WLS. Static would say a few words on occasion and at times was heard talking in the distance when he had no part in a program. Hay, another Hoosier born in Attica, Indiana, was named "World's Best Radio Announcer" in 1924, but the competition couldn't have been too stiff.

Hay billed himself as the "solemn old judge" despite the fact that he was neither old, a judge, nor solemn. Telling three lies in only three words was a remarkable feat. The name originated when he was a reporter for the Memphis Commercial-Appeal. He wrote a column about the city's night court and called it – what else but "The Solemn Old Judge."

When the newspaper experimented with a radio station, Hay was given the job of announcer. This led to him going to Chicago and WLS. At the time of his arrival there he was only 29 or 30. He was to play a key role in starting not only the National Barn Dance but the Grand Ole Opry in Nashville.

Although Static – the parrot, not the crackling noise that was an accepted nuisance in the early days of radio – was undoubtedly popular with listeners down on the farm, WLS also

The Not-So-Solemn Old Judge

broadcast programs of interest to more sophisticated listeners. Among them were speeches by President Calvin Coolidge, proving that Silent Cal wasn't always silent, and the welcoming ceremonies for Charles Lindbergh after his solo flight across the Atlantic.

There were dramatic serials as well. These would soon come to be known as soap operas because of the predominance of sponsors such as Lever Brothers and Proctor & Gamble. For nearly three decades radio listeners could spend the daylight hours with program after program "brought to you by . . ." Lifebouy, Rinso, Lux, Oxydol, Ivory and a long list of other products for either the bathroom or wash tub. If you didn't care for the tear-jerker playing on CBS you could switch to others on the NBC Red or Blue networks. The latter would become ABC in 1943.

There was comedy, too, and a pair of the acts heard on WLS in the 1920s would later, after leaving the station, became huge, nationwide hits. One was called "The Smith Family" and the other "Sam and Henry." Both ranked right along with "The Trietsch Brothers and Ward" in being quickly forgettable. A married couple, Marian and Jim Jordan, later dropped the Smith name in favor of "Fibber McGee and Molly." Freeman Gosden and Charles Correll did the same, ditching their blackface duo and achieving fame and fortune with a similar pair, "Amos 'n' Andy."

The station also broadcast the music of the Abe Lyman Orchestra and numerous other Chicago area bands as well as the homespun recitals of humorist Will Rogers. Another group of Hoosiers were popular performers on WLS, the barbershop quartet out of LaPorte known as the Maple City Four.

At times the radio audience was treated to – or tormented by – the fervent appeals of preachers to see the light, and don't forget to send money. Those forerunners of the television evangelists were quick to see an entirely new method of reaching out to people – more of them in a single broadcast than they could see face to face in a year of tent meetings and revivals.

So in the early years WLS provided a truly mixed bag of programming. Despite its success, changes were in the offing.

WLS **THE PRAIRIE FARMER STATION**
50,000 Watts   -   -   -   1200 Washington Blvd.
870 Kilocycles   -   -   Burridge D. Butler, Pres.

For more than 150 years the Prairie Farmer Magazine has played an important role in the lives of America's farmers and their families. In the 21st century Prairie Farmer also offers up-to-the-minute online news concerning the world of agriculture.

In 1928 it decided to try its hand at broadcast radio. The opportunity arose when officials at Sears Roebuck decided that selling merchandise, not operating a radio station, was the company's forte. The changeover took place on October 1 of that year.

While the station focused on the farmer and the things of importance to him such as weather forecasts as well as current market and produce reports, there were programs of interest to the city dweller as well. Broadcasts direct from the Chicago World's Fair of 1933, for example, and the ever-popular National Barn Dance. The mission never wavered, though, from being a friend to the farmer.

It was in 1928, too, that an odd switching around of frequencies took place that resulted in WLS having to share air time with rival WENR. The unusual setup continued until the early 1950s and was the cause of considerable bickering between the two stations. Eventually WLS would become a 50,000 watt, clear channel station.

A number of personalities, some remembered in the 21st century while others have been forgotten, enhanced their careers by moving from lesser-known stations to WLS. Among them were Patti Page, Andy Williams, Homer and Jethro, and George Goebel. Many others who gained a following on The National Barn Dance did the same.

What is arguably the most unforgettable broadcast in WLS history wasn't heard until the day following the event. This was because Herb Morrison, one of the station's newsmen, wasn't doing a live report as he described the fiery crash of the German dirigible Hindenburg at Lakehurst, New Jersey on May 6, 1937. His account, a radio classic, is still heard on recordings and occasionally a TV news show or documentary.

Morrison was experimenting with a technique for recording events in the field, something that would become commonplace in later years but was a pioneering endeavor at the time. An engineer from WLS preserved Morrison's words on a disk resembling an oversized phonograph record.

Many theories as to the cause of the Hindenburg disaster have been heard during the intervening years, yet the event is still shrouded in mystery. The giant airship, the pride of Hitler's Nazi Germany, was kept buoyant by flammable hydrogen-filled cells because the United States refused to sell helium to the oppressive government. As a result it was a disaster waiting to happen, although other German dirigibles, often called Zeppelins in honor of their originator, flew for many years without problems. Adding to the tenseness and suspense surrounding the crash, Morrison and his engineer were reportedly followed by Nazi SS men and were able to make their way back to Chicago only after eluding them.

So that, in brief, was what awaited Ken, Hezzie and Gabe when they made the trek from Fort Wayne to Chicago along U.S. Route 30. It wasn't a long drive, no more than three hours even if they stopped for coffee along the way, but it was the beginning of a journey that would lead them to fame, if not fortune. Before it ended it would take them across the country and across the Atlantic.

When WLS first went on the air the boys were touring the United States with Ezra Buzzington's Rube Band. More than anything else it was the movies, the talkies, that drove vaudeville from the theaters of America. Ironically, as the Hoosier Hot Shots they would in a few short years return to the theaters in movies of their own.

Did they realize when they crossed the state line on the drive to Chicago that they were not only leaving their beloved Indiana behind but would return on only rare occasions? It's unlikely that they did. Had they known, would it have changed their minds about making the trip? That's even more unlikely. But at least one, Gabe Ward, left a large piece of his heart behind. His love for the Hoosier State would never diminish.

Program WLS Program

NATIONAL BARN DANCE

FIRST SHOW
7:30 to 9:30 p. m. CST

ALL TIME IS
CURTISS Candy Time
Bar. Babe Ruth Candy

SECOND SHOW
10:00 to 12:00 p. m. CST

Masters of Ceremonies:

JACK STILWILL   JOE KELLY   JACK HOLDEN   BILL McCLUSKY

WLS welcomes you to the National Barn Dance—a feature that millions of radio listeners in the United States and Canada have enjoyed since April, 1924. Not only does the Barn Dance reach the WLS audience, but the hour from 8:00 to 9:00 goes on a coast-to-coast NBC network of 69 stations. So many desired to witness the performances that the Barn Dance "moved" to the Eighth Street Theater in March, 1932. The entertainers who appear before you have become favorites of the air because they are just "home folks," striving to do their best to lighten your cares by bringing you wholesome fun and entertainment. They hope that you will enjoy their show from the ringing of the first cowbell until "Good Night Ladies."

PRESENTATION OF ACTS .... ENTIRE COMPANY

DeKOCK SISTERS .... Caroline and Mary Jane
    Buy these by Curtiss Sisterhoods here—they are rich in Rhttrrss

CHUCK, RAY & CHRISTINE .... Vocal Trio
    Chuck Hayton, Roy Perez, Christine Erickson.
    For energy, for enjoyment, make Babe Ruth candy a daily habit.

OTTO & HIS NOVELODEONS .... Instrumental and Vocal Novelties
    Tip Blume (Otto), George Duff, Ted Gilmore, Russ Harvey, Art Wenzel

LULU BELLE .... "The Belle of the Barn Dance"

"SKYLAND SCOTTY" WISEMAN .... Singer of Mountain Folk Songs

THE NATIONAL BARN DANCE

What must the boys have been thinking when they walked out on the WLS stage for the first time? Entertaining wasn't new to them, of course, not after years on vaudeville and having their own show on WOWO radio. But this was different. Now they would be heard throughout the country so there had to have been at least a little thrill, a touch of excitement to the experience.

EVERY SATURDAY NIGHT
Alka-Seltzer
NATIONAL BARN DANCE
with
EDDIE PEABODY
PAT BUTTRAM — JOE KELLY
HOOSIER HOT SHOTS
KDKA WBEN WGY WTAM WHAM
WLW WORK WGAL—9 P.M., EST

What song or songs did they play that first night? Did Ken say, "Are you ready, Hezzie?" Very likely, although the program wasn't recorded so chances are no one will ever know. Excerpts from a few original shows are available on tape or disc but none, at least that have come to light, of that first appearance by the Hoosier Hot Shots.

Their arrival in Chicago was perfectly timed. In 1932 what for eight years had been the WLS Barn Dance became the National Barn Dance when it was picked up by the NBC Blue network and broadcast coast to coast. That was the year before the boys arrived on the scene. They had been playing with the Buzzington band at the time the program made its debut on the night of April 19, 1924, the first Saturday the station was on the air. The initial broadcast wasn't much to shout about, just some local talent with the emphasis on fiddlers from the Appalachian hills. George D. Hay, the Solemn Old Judge, handled the announcing. The response was immediate and highly favorable.

Not everyone was impressed, however. Officials at Sears Roebuck were horrified by what they termed "disgraceful low-brow music." They seemed to forget that the very audience they were appealing to was comprised for the most part of unsophisticated, basically uneducated, low-brow farm dwellers. Those tuned in had heard their kind of music and they didn't hesitate in making it known. Told of the congratulatory telegrams and phone calls, the big shots at Sears saw the light. The Barn Dance, later to become the National Barn Dance, was established as a regular Saturday night feature on WLS.

BRADLEY KINCAID

A number of performers quickly established themselves as Barn Dance fixtures. Among them was Bradley Kincaid, although a few years passed before he joined the show. Kincaid was different in that he stuck to the old favorites from the hill country. He didn't just sing them; he went far back in the Kentucky hill country in search of them. His determination to be authentic rather than a singer of current hits allowed listeners to hear songs that otherwise would have remained locked away in the minds of men who would never have dreamed of taking them to the outside world, a place totally alien to them.

Arguably the best of the songs introduced by Kincaid, or at least the best known, was *On Top of Old Smokey*. Years later The Weavers recording of the song became a huge hit on the pop music charts. A few other Kincaid discoveries were *Sweet Betsy From Pike, Bury Me Beneath the Willow, Little Red Rooster and the Old Black Hen, Little Darling Don't Say We Are Through,* and *Old Dan Tucker.*

One of Kincaid's records that attracted a wide audience was *The Legend of the Robin's Red Breast*. Because of the story it told, the song was a favorite among church-goers. On the flip side was one this writer particularly enjoyed, *I Traced Her Little Footprints in the Snow*. It told the story of a young man who searched for and found Nellie, the love of his life, when she was lost in the woods. It does seem, though, that Nellie was not too bright or she might have retraced her own footprints and ended up back where she started. That would have spoiled a good story, of course.

Many of the early performers on the Barn Dance would achieve fame and sometimes fortune in later years. Chief among them was Gene Autry. The singing cowboy would star in many movies and had a number of hit records. His *Rudolph the Red Nosed Reindeer* is still heard on radio during every Christmas season. Two men who would later be his movie sidekicks, Smiley Burnette and Pat Buttram, also were members of the Barn Dance crew.

Gabe, Ken and Hezzie benefited from their acquaintance-ship with Autry. He starred in the first movie in which the Hot Shots appeared. This led to another twenty or so films and as a result they packed up and moved to California. That was years in the future, however, when they first arrived in Chicago.

Most of the Barn Dance stars, big names in the business at the time, are forgotten in the 21st Century. Two of the most popular, Lulu Belle and Scotty, began as single acts but their boy-meets-girl stage romance carried over into real life and they were married. Program officials feared the marriage would spoil their make-believe role as sweethearts. Instead it made them more popular than ever. Scotty, an accomplished songwriter, wrote what became a country classic, *Have I Told*

LULU BELLE & SCOTTY

You Lately That I Love You. Did he perhaps have Lulu Belle in mind when he began composing?

Lulu Belle and Scotty were on the show for many years, as was a fellow called Arkie, the Arkansas Woodchopper. Patsy Montana, Kurt Massey, Rex Allen and Max Terhune went on to star in movies. Red Foley became a country music icon, as did Jimmie Rodgers and Bill Monroe. Pie Plant Pete had his own long- running radio show. A young lady named Sally Foster sang on many Barn Dance shows. She enjoyed singing the sweet, old-fashioned songs. Eddy Peabody was known as the nation's leading banjo player.

Several Barn Dance regulars became leading lights of popular music. Henry Burr was an established concert singer long before he was heard on the Barn Dance. In 1941-42, Billy Murray, a recording star for decades, substituted for Burr. Andy Williams was on the show as part of the Williams Brothers act. Les Paul, of the trio bearing his name, later teamed with Mary Ford to record many hits in the pop field. George Goebel played a ukulele as a child star on the show and went on to becoming a leading comedian on television.

Homer and Jethro, late comers to the Barn Dance, took their act to television with great success. There were others who enjoyed at least modest popularity after their days on the National Barn Dance and several of the men who operated behind the scenes were seen as leaders in their respective fields. Among them was John Lair, who worked closely with Bradley Kincaid in making some of the songs he discovered deep in the hills of Kentucky suitable for a wider audience.

Lair also discovered Lulu Belle when she was working as a store clerk.

Then there was Uncle Ezra, the Jumpin' Jenny Wren, who supposedly broadcast from his "powerful five-watter down in Rosedale, the friendly little city." Uncle Ezra, whose real name was Patrick Barrett, always rushed in late saying, "Hain't missed nuthin' – have I?" His homespun philosophy routine was as popular with listeners as any act on the show.

UNCLE EZRA

Uncle Ezra's Rosedale was in Southern Illinois, but in a remote area of Indiana's Parke County there is a small settlement known as Rosedale. It's residents felt certain that Uncle Ezra really had them in mind as the friendly little city. They liked our boys so much that when it came time for the Rosedale High School basketball team to choose a nickname, Hot Shots was selected. It continued in use until the late 1980s when the school became part of a consolidation.

Despite the show's popularity, no one made much money from performing on the Barn Dance. Five to ten dollars a night was the average pay, but only after the program was well established. Reportedly in the early years of the show nearly 200 bands and other musical acts made regular appearances on the program without receiving a dime. As the years rolled by a few were paid a small amount by sponsors but their real money came from personal appearances. In an interview with Kenneth E. Baughman many years later, Gene Autry said, "We played most of the theaters and some auditoriums and local fairs all the way from Wisconsin and the Upper Peninsula of Michigan to Indiana and all over Illinois and Iowa . . ."

In a letter, Gabe Ward told of similar engagements but also said the Hot Shots would show up wherever crowds gathered just as they had done while at WOWO in Fort Wayne. When there was an opportunity to win fans and build a following the Hot Shots were quick to seize it.

Small town Hoosier boys they might be, but Gabe, Ken and Hezzie were intelligent enough to know that promoting was a major part of their job even when there was no immediate return for a day's work. In the long run there would be, so such off-the-clock efforts were worthwhile. Perhaps that was one thing that helped separate them from the pack of imitators and acts that might be big on home turf but would never go beyond that.

As might have been anticipated, fans wanted to see the show in person and only a hundred or so could be accommodated in the studio. In 1931 the Barn Dance began staging the broadcast at the 1,200 seat Eighth Street Theatre at 8th Street and Wabash Avenue in Chicago. Even that fell far short of meeting the demand for tickets. At times people lined up for hours or even arrived the night before. Some, apparently fearing the doors would be opened and it would turn into a first come, first served affair, did this even when they already possessed tickets guaranteeing them reserved seats. Throngs of

fans hoping they might somehow get inside the theatre milled about on the street outside. There were two shows every Saturday night, each different than the other, and the house was always sold out for both performances. Over the course of its twenty-six year run at the theatre nearly three million people attended the shows.

A number of announcers followed George D. Hay as emcee of the Barn Dance. One of the most popular was Joe Kelly, who would open the performance while ringing a cowbell. He began his duties at WLS as "Jolly Joe" on a morning program for kids. Later he was quizmaster on The Quiz Kids, a show featuring juveniles who knew the answer to nearly any question. Millions of listeners tuned in every week. There was more than a little irony in Kelly getting the job sought by many others because he had dropped out of grade school at the age of eight.

JOE KELLY

Countless imitators of the National Barn Dance sprang up during the grim years of the 1930s when Americans hungered for anything cheerful that would transport them from the world of reality even if only for a few hours. One that has survived into the 21st century is the Jamboree on radio station WWVA in Wheeling, West Virginia. Listeners in Ohio, Western Pennsylvania and WWVA's home state have been enjoying country music every Saturday night since 1933 aside from the World War II years when travel restrictions forced it off the air.

Herb Howard, who directed the National Barn Dance for five years, later started the Missouri Valley Barn Dance and served as producer and director.

It wasn't a spin-off of the National Barn Dance, but the roots of the Renfro Valley Barn Dance can be traced to the eight years John Lair spent at WLS. The man who helped Bradley Kincaid with the real hillbilly music he found in the hills of Kentucky was a native of the Bluegrass State himself. Lair was one of those rare men who had a big dream and actually saw it fulfilled and live on for decades after his own death. He started his own radio show, first in Cincinnati, then Dayton and finally Louisville, with the goal of making it true to

71

JOHN LAIR

the folk music of his home state rather than the variety style of programming heard on WLS. After years of work on the project and with some timely help from residents of the area, the Renfro Valley Barn Dance had a home of its own that still continues to offer regular programs although not on radio. There is much more than just country music at the entertainment center that draws crowds from throughout the country, including a book and music store. There also is a recording studio where anyone, for a price, can put their own music on a compact disc.

There were many more live country music shows on radio during that era, even one in New York City. Most have faded into history. One that has not can also be traced back to WLS and the Solemn Old Judge, George D. Hay.

On October 5, 1925, a year and a half after the National Barn Dance was first broadcast, a new station went on the air in Nashville. Hay was among the guests invited to take part in the opening ceremonies. The call letters of the station, WSM, stood for "We Shield Millions," the slogan of the National Life and Accident Insurance Company, sponsors of the venture. Edwin W. Craig, son of the insurance company's president, was in charge of the radio station.

Craig apparently was impressed by Hay's background because he offered him the job of program director and Hay, casting solemnity aside, leaped at the opportunity even though at the beginning the station had a range of only a few miles. It also lacked a country music program but Hay soon corrected that oversight. The first show consisted of nothing more than fiddle playing by an old fellow called Uncle Jimmy Thompson. As had been the case at WLS, telegrams from enthusiastic listeners quickly began pouring into the station.

The show, called the WSM Barn Dance became a Saturday night feature. The first real star of the program was Uncle Dave Macon, a singer and banjo player. There seemed to be no shortage of uncles in the Nashville area and Hay rounded up other local talent as well. For three years the program continued to grow with Hay doing the announcing. Then on the night of December 8, 1928 an event occurred that would have a lasting impact on the world of music.

For an hour preceding the WSM Barn Dance the station broadcast an NBC network program of classical music under noted director Walter Damrosch. Operatic selections were included. When it ended, the Solemn Old Judge said, "For the past hour we have been listening to music taken largely from Grand Opera. From now on we will present the Grand Ole Opry."

And thus was christened what would become the longest lasting and most famous of all country music shows on radio. Folks in Nashville may not like to admit it, but its roots are firmly planted in the WLS National Barn Dance, the first of such programs.

GEORGE D. HAY – INDEED THE SOLEMN OLD JUDGE

A TYPICAL SATURDAY NIGHT PROGRAM ON
THE WLS NATIONAL BARN DANCE

**Appearing This Week on WLS &
The National Barn Dance
September 12, 1936**

06:00 PM
06:00 PM;

Prairie Ramblers and Patsy Montana

06:15 PM
06:15 PM;

Roy Anderson, baritone · Ralph Emerson, organ

06:30 PM
06:30 PM;
Keystone Steel and Wire Co.
Lulu Belle

07:00 PM
07:00 PM;
Murphy's Products Co.
Hometowners · Grace Wilson · Prairie Ramblers and Patsy Montana · The
Hilltoppers · Otto's Novelodeons · Pat Buttram · Winnie, Lou & Sally

07:30 PM
07:30 PM;
Alka-Seltzer
Uncle Ezra · Maple City Four · Verne, Lee and mary · Hoosier Hot Shots · Henry
Burr · Sally Foster · Otto & His Novelodeons · Lucille Long · Lulu Belle · Skyland
Scotty · and other Hayloft favorites · with Joe Kelly as master of ceremonies

08:30 PM
08:30 PM;
Gillette
Hilltoppers · Red Foley

08:45 PM
08:45 PM;
Conkey
Henry Hornsbuckle · Four Hired Hands · George Goebel

09:00 PM
09:00 PM;

including Magnolia Time

09:45 PM
09:45 PM;

Varied Features until Midnight · Prairie Ramblers and Patsy Montana · The
Hilltoppers · Hometowners Quartet · Christine · Otto & His Novelodeons · Henry ·
George Goebel · Lulu Belle & Scotty · Grace Wilson · Hooseir Sod Busters · Eddie
Allan · Arkie · Four Hired Hands · and many others

THE HOT SHOTS MAKE A HIT

Conditions were steadily improving in most of the country by 1933. The economy, such as it was, had bottomed out and now there were numerous signs that the corner, while not yet turned, was drawing nearer. That was an oft-heard slogan, "Prosperity is just around the corner." The feeling of hopelessness that prevailed from 1930 through 1932 had been replaced by one of cautious optimism. Life was still hard for the majority of Americans, downright dreadful for a great many, but the grim-faced Hoover was gone and his replacement in the White House, Franklin D. Roosevelt, was a man with a ready smile and words of hope.

"There is nothing to fear but fear itself" struck a welcome chord in the minds of people eager to start the upward climb. It wasn't all talk and smiles, of course. New programs were begun that put breadwinners back to work. Not the work they had enjoyed prior to the Crash, not work that paid a comparable amount of money, but work that paid the rent and put food on the table. It may not have been much, but it was a start. Hope for the future was restored along with the pride that had taken a woeful beating when a man's kids were going to bed hungry and his wife's eyes held an ever-present look of reproach..

All things considered, it was an ideal time for the Hoosier Hot Shots to burst upon the national scene. For many there was a reason to smile again and the boys offered them an opportunity to turn the smile into a laugh. For those who had yet to find cause for even a smile, the antics and toe-tapping sound of the Hot Shots provided one.

"What we had," Gabe Ward wrote decades later, "was a product called stupid."

Perhaps it was, but there are times when people enjoy stupid. For proof, check the majority of television sitcoms. Still, Gabe knew there was more to it than that. There's enjoyment, and it was obvious to listeners that here were three guys having a heck of a good time doing what they loved to do. There's skill, and acting silly requires a great deal of it or it quickly becomes tiresome. There's ability, and people knew that before you can do crazy things with musical instruments you must know how to play them properly.

There was one more requirement: To do the things the Hot Shots did, to play the music they played in the way they did, you had to be genuine. You can't fake it, at least not for long. Audiences saw them for what they were, unpretentious, wholesome, fun-loving young fellows from the heartland. The kind of men you'd trust to hold your wallet or take your daughter out on a date.

The Hot Shots first Chicago appearances, Gabe said, came on Uncle Ezra's radio show. "Radio station E.Z.R.A. down in Coles County, Illinois was entirely mythical and was really a soap opera. Pat Barrett was Uncle Ezra P. Watters, the Jumpin' Jenny Wren. Folks took it to their hearts, sent in money to the depicted characters, and so much mail came that the post office set up a substation near Mattoon. The song *Rosedale, Everyone's Hometown* was our sign-off each time. I did sub-tone clarinet behind Ezra's recitation."

Despite the carload of competition, the Hoosier Hot Shots were an immediate hit on the National Barn Dance. The time would come when Roosevelt scheduled his fireside chats with the nation right after the Hot Shots were on the air because he knew that would guarantee millions were already tuned in.

The Hot Shots soon had a sponsor for their 8:30 p.m. slot on the Barn Dance. "Who else would we work for," wrote Gabe, "but Dr. Miles Laboratories in Elkhart (Indiana), the makers of Alka-Seltzer. We were their boys. We started with a handshake and soon had a contract worth $1,000 each Saturday night live from the Eighth Street Theater in Chicago. Admission was 85 cents to see those broadcasts. There were 1,200 seats and they were sold out weeks in advance."

It wasn't long after arriving in Chicago that the boys decided they needed another man, a bass player to fill out the sound and maintain the tempo. Ken was skillful on the tuba, but during the preceding decade it had gone out of fashion, replaced by the string bass. Then, too, Ken was too busy with other things to haul out the tuba he so dearly loved.

What was needed, they decided was a string bass player, but not just anyone who wandered in off the street. He had to be a man of similar nature, not some old grump or a man who would just stand there like a stick while plucking his instrument. One name leaped to all minds: Frank Kettering.

Frank had spent three years with Ezra Buzzington's Rube Band so they knew him well. They also knew there had never been any stick-in-the-muds with Buzzington so he was just the sort of man they were looking for. On top of that he also was an expert on the piccolo, flute, guitar, banjo, piano and organ. Some of those instruments would never be part of the act but being able to play them meant he was a first rate musician. He had been playing the fife before audiences since the age of five and while in high school he had even played with John Philip Sousa's band when it was in Monmouth, Illinois, Frank's hometown. You couldn't have much better credentials..

So the boys sent out a call to Monmouth and in August of 1934 Kettering joined them in Chicago. It wasn't long before he was helping out Ken by doing some of the arranging and in time even wrote, or helped write, a few of their songs. For the Hoosier Hot Shots, Frank Kettering was a perfect fit. He might not have been a Hoosier, but Illinois is right next door.

NOW A FOURSOME – FRANK, GABE, KEN, HEZZIE

77

Like Hezzie, Ken and Gabe, Frank was married. The story of how it came about was a bit bizarre. While the Buzzington band was playing in Greensburg, Pa., Frank had a date with a girl named Dorothy Kosko. While they were out, his hotel room was robbed so he had to stick around town for a few weeks. By the time he rejoined the band, Frank and Dorothy were married.

It quickly became apparent that the time had come for the boys to make a permanent move to Chicago. Gabe and Marguerite bought a house on the west side of the city for $16,000. That amount of money would have bought a real showplace during the Depression. One of their many houseguests was Gabe's old boss, Mark Schaefer, better known as Ezra Buzzington. At the time Schaefer was retired and living on his farm near Farmland, Indiana. Gabe often mentioned Schaefer's great baritone singing voice. Before starting his band he sang accompaniments to silent movies.

Ken and Hezzie also settled in with houses of their own and Hot Shot babies came along to add a little more responsibility to their lives. Through personal appearances the boys were doing as well or better financially than they had even during the years on vaudeville. By no means were they getting rich but the $250 a week from Alka-Seltzer for each of them added to what they were making from personal appearances meant they were earning more money than the majority of Americans.

Still, they never lost touch with their roots, never lost the common touch. Gabe wrote, "Playing charity events, hospitals, convalescent homes and so forth put us in touch with Lonely Street." Fortunately decades would go by before any of them had to walk that street but they never lost sight of the fact that it existed. For now there were good times to enjoy and they did so to the fullest.

As time went on all of the boys acted as goodwill ambassadors and worked hard at winning friends who would become fans. Gabe continued to serve as unofficial public relations man because he enjoyed working with members of the press. None of them ever was at a loss for words but Gabe was especially talented in that respect. Another of his unofficial jobs was teaching Hezzie all the new arrangements.

Gabe never lost his affection for Miles Laboratories and Alka-Seltzer. His association with the company began long before the radio days when as a boy he delivered the Dr. Miles Almanac in Alexandria for several years. Later he paid visits to the Pedler and Conn Instrument plants that, like Miles Laboratories, were located in Elkhart. Long years after his association with the firm he fondly mentioned Alka-Seltzer in letters. Gabe wasn't a man to forget a pleasant association, whether it was with a person or a sponsor.

Early in 1937 the Prairie Farmer magazine reported that the Hoosier Hot Shots were going to California to appear in the movie *Mountain Music* starring comedians Bob Burns and Martha Raye. Burns was another old vaudeville performer who had hit it big on radio. For a number of years he appeared on the Bing Crosby Show where his down home Arkansas humor proved popular. So did the homemade musical instrument he called a bazooka.

The bazooka was so important to his act that Burns copyrighted the name in 1920. During the early stages of World War II that did not stop soldiers from calling a new tube-like anti-tank rocket launcher that resembled his

79

instrument a bazooka. The name stuck. Long after most Americans had forgotten Bob Burns the majority of them knew exactly what a bazooka was, although not the original version invented and copyrighted by the man who played it on stage, screen and radio.

Martha Raye was a loud, outgoing woman whose mouth was unusually large. That was part of her comedy routine and rare was the show on radio when it was not mentioned. It never failed to draw laughter from the studio audience and listeners at home. In the 21st century it likely would be considered politically incorrect.

But the report that the Hoosier Hot Shots would be in *Mountain Music* was false. Nowhere do they appear in the film's credits, Gabe said they were not in the film and when they really did travel to Hollywood several years later a newspaper columnist wrote that it was their first appearance on the coast.

KEN JUST COULDN'T RESIST HAULING OUT HIS BELOVED TUBA AS FRANK WATCHES GABE CLOWN AROUND WITH HEZZIE

From their very first appearance on the National Barn Dance there was a demand for Hoosier Hot Shots records. Columbia was quick to take advantage of this. Beginning in 1934 and continuing for the following seven years the boys made frequent visits to the recording studios. The vast majority of the discs were released on one or several of Columbia's numerous subsidiaries including Vocalion, Okeh, Melotone and Banner, the labels best known by the record-buying public. In the discography found here only Vocalion numbers are listed because one was assigned to nearly every Hot Shot recording.

The Hot Shots recorded eight songs during their first studio session on November 13, 1934. Probably the most popular were *Sentimental Gentleman From Georgia* and *Whistlin' Joe From Kokomo*. On the flip side of *Sentimental Gentleman* was *Farmer Gray*, another song often associated with the boys. *Oakville Twister* was one of many Hoosier Hot Shots originals recorded over the years. Tiny Oakville lay just a short distance south of the Trietsch homestead near Muncie.

Nineteen songs recorded by the boys in 1935 were released that year, but it should be kept in mind that recording dates and release dates do not always coincide. An odd number of recordings in a particular year doesn't mean an artist or artists appeared on only a single side of a record. Nor were all songs recorded eventually released.

Sometimes singers and musical groups want to record a song but are denied the opportunity. A classical example came when polka band leader Frankie Yankovic asked to record *Just Because* but company officials didn't like it. Finally after doing sixteen recordings one day the band was allowed to do *Just Because*. It turned out to be one of the all-time great polka hits and was forever linked to the Yankovic band, proving that studio employees, like editors, often make mistakes.

Three of the 1935 songs became Hot Shot classics: *I Like Bananas Because They Have No Bones*, *Them Hill-Billies Are Mountain Williams Now* and *Back Home Again In Indiana*. Gabe Ward was credited with writing another, *I Wish That I Was Back In Indiana*. In time it would come to express his outlook on life.

While none of the twenty-three 1936 songs are recalled as Hoosier Hot Shot classics, many proved quite popular. Among them were *I Like Mountain Music, That's What I Learned In College* and one of my personal favorites, *Wah-Hoo!*

The boys recorded nine songs at two sessions early in 1937 and two became big hits: *Breezin' Along With The Breeze* and *The Coat And Pants Do All The Work But The Vest Gets All The Gravy.* Late in the year *Breezin'* was the first Hot Shot recording to appear on the Pop Music Chart of hit records.

Production picked up again in 1938 when twenty recordings were released. Two of them, *Red Hot Fannie* and *The Man With The Whiskers,* made the Pop Music Charts. The Hot Shots recorded a number of pop hits and jazz favorites.

In 1939 another record, *Annabelle,* appeared on the Pop Music Charts. Five years would go by before it happened again. The boys also recorded what proved to be one of their classics, *From The Indies To The Andes In His Undies.* Again they recorded a number of pop hits and revivals of old songs.

The twenty-eight songs recorded by the Hot Shots in 1940 was their largest number in a single year. None were huge hits but many were well received. The same was true in 1941 when their eighteen records were popular but not exceptionally so. Best remembered may be *Since We Put A Radio Out In The Hen House.* Popular hits of the day and remakes of old favorites continued to be the mainstays for the boys.

Big changes occurred in 1942, the first full year the United States was involved in World War II. The Hot Shots made only three records and none in 1943 because of the musicians strike. In any event, their focus was beginning to shift during that period although they continued on with their radio work just as before. However, their appearance in the 1939 movie *In Old Monterey* along with the nation's preoccupation with the war created an entirely different atmosphere. The Great Depression was over so it wasn't just the Hoosier Hot Shots who were charting a new course. Doors that had been firmly closed for a decade suddenly were wide open and the boys were on the verge of entering one. Their lives would never again be the same.

OTHER HOOSIERS MAKE THE NEWS

The Hot Shots weren't the only Hoosiers making news during the dark days of the 1930s. One was entertaining readers from coast to coast with daily columns in Scripps-Howard newspapers. Others were making headlines robbing banks

Ernie Pyle, the writer, was born August 3, 1900 at the family farm just outside the little town of Dana a few miles east of the Illinois state line. That's flatland farm country little different than that where Gabe, Ken and Hezzie had spent their formative years. While Ernie appreciated music, he didn't share their passion for it. Instead he was pretty much your average kid of that era just having a good time and, perhaps unwittingly, storing up memories that one day would be put down on paper for others to share and enjoy.

There was the time, for example, when his father decided to fix an annoying squeak on the family car. He wasn't quite sure about what needed oil and what didn't so he oiled the brakes, then a little later was surprised when the pedal went right to the floor and he drove through the plate glass window of a store in Dana.

Ernie, who grew up to be a small man with a big grin, studied journalism at Indiana University. He wrote for the *Indiana Daily Student,* at times holding various editorial positions including city editor. While he learned all the rules of grammar, his writing would always retain a bit of Hoosier simplicity and style. That made it popular with readers everywhere.

One of Ernie's friends at IU was Paige Cavanaugh, who later made beautiful music with the trio bearing his name. Another student, Hoagy Carmichael, played piano at a local hangout and Ernie sometimes attended dances so music played a role in his life, though not a major one. A few years later while working at the Washington *News* he and some of the other reporters and deskmen would occasionally do a little singing while swigging bathtub gin at a party. Ernie had a decent voice and often sang one of his favorites, *Back Home Again In Indiana*.

After a short stint at the newspaper in LaPorte, Indiana, he moved on to Washington. As so often happens, his skill as a copyreader kept him working at a desk job that failed to take advantage of his real talent, which was writing. Ernie's skills in the craft were truly uncommon.. He could paint word pictures that made a reader see what Ernie had seen and he had an ability to describe both the good and bad times in the lives of ordinary people in a way that enabled readers to share their joy or feel their pain. This rare skill led to an assignment that made him the envy of every reporter in the land. He could start out in his car, usually accompanied by his wife Jerry, and go anywhere in the country that he felt like visiting. Once there, Ernie (photo at left) could stay for as long or short a time as he wished and write a daily column about the places he saw or the people he met.

He didn't write every day, though. Instead he would gather material for a couple of weeks and then hole up in a quiet place, preferably a state park, and turn out fourteen or fifteen columns. His bosses at Scripps-Howard didn't care how he did it just so long as the columns kept coming on time.

One of his most memorable pieces was written after a visit home to see his parents in Dana. For some reason he took his father's shotgun out to the barnyard and came face to face with a groundhog. Farmers consider them a nuisance so Ernie shot it, then was dismayed to discover it was a female and pregnant. The rest of the day he was troubled by the memory of the startled look on the groundhog's face when it discovered it was cut off from its burrow. He couldn't get it off his mind and wrote that while he was thinking about it that evening, "I just felt like hell."

Then there was the time he checked into a lodge in a remote area out west. He wanted to stretch his legs so he asked the lady at the desk if there were any snakes in the vicinity. Assured that there were none, he set off down a trail. He had gone only a short distance when he came to a stream and there coiled on a rock was a snake. Ernie wrote that he leaped back and gave his special snake-fright yell, then hurried back to the lodge and berated the woman for misleading him. She told him it wasn't a poisonous snake so he said, "I'm not afraid of being bitten by a snake, I'm afraid of *seeing* a snake."

The Pyle's, both Ernie and Jerry, had one failing that was shared by many in the newspaper business – they drank too much. It rarely interfered with his work but on at least one occasion Jerry spent time drying out in a sanitarium.

Ernie Pyle's plush assignment came to an end when the United States entered World War II. He switched to being a war correspondent and once again set himself apart from the other reporters in North Africa, Sicily, Italy and then France after D-Day. Rather than staying in a press tent well behind the lines and waiting to be handed press releases or for an occasional interview with a colonel or a general, Ernie wandered alone up to the front. There he would talk with the privates and sergeants in infantry rifle companies, always taking down names and including them in his dispatches. He visited artillery cannoneers, combat engineers and men in other units but his first love was always the infantrymen because "they live so horribly and die so horribly."

In no time the stories filed by Ernie Pyle became the favorites not only of the people back home but the soldiers and sailors in every theater of operations. In the opinion of the fighting men, he alone told the story as it really was taking place.

Early on the morning of July 25, 1944 I was out on a dirt road beside our company area in Normandy when a Jeep approached from the rear. It pulled up beside me and the driver asked for directions to the regiment directly ahead. I was slow in answering because slumped in the back seat was Ernie Pyle. He had the thousand-yard stare of an infantryman who had been too long in combat and looked weary enough to have been right at home in a rifle company or a combat exhaustion center.

I hurried back and told the others I had just seen Ernie Pyle. They just grinned and said, "Yeah, sure you did." I was proven right, though, because he wrote a moving column about the huge air raid in front of our position that day and how he had been with our division as it took place. It can still be found in the book *Brave Men*.

Ernie later went to the Pacific and was killed by a sniper only months before the war ended. The small house in Dana where he grew up is now a museum dedicated to the memory of the greatest of all war correspondents and truly one of America's outstanding writers.

And then there was that other famous Hoosier, John Dillinger. Like the Hot Shots and Ernie Pyle, he had grown up in Central Indiana. For fifteen or sixteen years he lived in Indianapolis, where he was born June 22, 1903, and then a little to the southwest in the small town of Mooresville.

That was one thing the five of them had in common – all were small town boys. They were roughly the same age and all possessed a dry, Hoosier-style sense of humor. Had they spent time together on, say, a camping trip they would have gotten along famously. Each would have enjoyed the stories told by the others and they might even have joined in singing *Back Home Again In Indiana* or *On The Banks Of The Wabash*.

They also shared a common interest in people, although Dillinger had an odd manner of showing it at times. The one vital way in which he differed from the others was his intense craving for excitement, his contempt for the conventional way of life. Still, one could hardly call the lives of the other four conventional. He did have a deep sense of loyalty to friends

86

and family and his own brand of honor. Despite his reputation he was not a vicious man by nature, although he could resort to violence when it was necessary for self preservation. He claimed he never killed a man even though he was charged with killing an East Chicago policeman during a bank robbery. The evidence, although confusing, doesn't seem to back up his contention that he was a thousand miles away at the time.

John Dillinger could be the poster boy for those who insist an unhappy childhood totally lacking in love is the cause of wild, rebellious actions that can lead to a life of crime. His mother died when he was three so for a year he was "raised" by a much older sister, then she married and left. His father, a prosperous grocer, was a cold, religious man who believed any show of affection was unmanly. Therefore young Johnnie received none. When he was nine his father remarried but the boy and his step-mother never developed a close relationship.

Young Johnnie became increasingly rebell-ious and developed a sarcastic, one-sided grin that was displayed more and more frequently. His only confidantes were a couple of other boys who had similar problems at home. With them he en-

A YOUTHFUL DILLINGER

gaged in some wild escapades but nothing that led to serious trouble with the law or provided a clue to his eventual career in crime. His activities did lead his father to move the family, if it could be called that, to Mooresville when John was sixteen. He felt that farm life and being away from the city would reform John. He was enrolled in high school, where he was well behaved but never studied and had nothing other than failing

grades. When asked to come to the school to discuss the situation, his father claimed to be too busy.

During the next year or so he was married, perhaps twice, enlisted in the Navy but didn't like being ordered around by so many people and deserted, then was given a dishonorable discharge.

John's first serious encounter with the law came when he tried to rob a Mooresville grocer at gunpoint as the man walked along a street. During the course of a scuffle he hit the grocer on the head with a bolt he was carrying. He was arrested and the county prosecutor promised him a suspended sentence if he pleaded guilty. The prosecutor told John he didn't need a lawyer. His father, as might be expected, was too busy to attend John's hearing in court. Ignoring the plea agreement, the judge handed him a ten- to twenty-year sentence at the state reformatory in Pendleton. It was a bitter, angry young John Dillinger who heard the gate slam shut behind him.

HARRY PIERPONT

At Pendleton he made two close friends, both of them fellow Hoosiers. Harry Pierpont was a strapping, handsome man bearing a striking resemblance to the actor Paul Newman when Newman was young. I once talked with a cousin of his who had met him when she was a young girl. This was at a family reunion near Muncie and she remembered him as having the most brilliant blue eyes she would ever see. Although only a year older than Dillinger, Pierpont was at Pendleton for the serious offense of having robbed a bank in Kokomo. Despite his good looks and a doting mother, Pierpont had a vicious streak that allowed him to kill without compunction.

Oddly enough, Pierpont hated John's other close friend at Pendleton, Homer Van Meter. Although hard as nails, Van Meter, who came from Fort Wayne, was a comedian with the ability to throw himself completely out of joint. He did this frequently to amuse other prisoners. Perhaps it was this sort of behavior that alienated the deadly serious Pierpont.

Both of them soon were transferred to the Indiana State penitentiary at Michigan City for separate acts of disobedience. This led Dillinger, an excellent baseball player and shortstop on the Pendleton team, to ask for a transfer to Michigan City when he was turned down for parole despite having been a model prisoner for years. At about the same time his wife divorced him.

At Michigan City, Dillinger found himself among hardened, mature criminals and life was difficult for him. As time went on, though, he became known as a good friend to other inmates and a skilled worker in the shirt shop. A gradual transformation from wild young kid to steady, reliable man took place.

With a parole likely in the near future, he was offered the chance to be the outside man on a breakout planned by Pierpont and his gang: John Hamilton, Charlie Makley and Russell Clark. Hamilton was a chance-taking daredevil while Makley was an intelligent, smooth operator capable of gaining the trust of just about anyone. He was chiefly responsible for the elaborate escape plans.

Money would be needed in order to smuggle guns into the prison so Dillinger was given a list of banks and businesses to rob, a list drawn up by Pierpont's group. This was in 1933, however, and the list was badly outdated because of the Wall Street Crash. Dillinger was coached by another potential escapee, Walter Dietrich. He had learned the way of approaching a bank robbery as you would a military operation from Herman K. Lamm, who had successfully plied the trade for thirteen years.

Following his parole on May 10, 1933, Dillinger assumed the role of model citizen in Mooresville just as he had been coached to do by Pierpont and Van Meter. The people who believed he was a changed man were unaware he had already contacted a second-tier criminal named Noble Claycomb, one of those on the list of potential associates given him by Pierpont. They, along with a William Shaw, robbed an Indianapolis supermarket. Other robberies were quickly staged, sometimes with Claycomb, Shaw or Harry Copeland of Muncie. They rented rooms in a house in Muncie but the landlady tipped off the cops because she knew a man – Dillinger – who wore a new shirt from McNaughton's Department Store every day had to be an outlaw. The others were captured but Dillinger, who was just returning to the house, made his escape by backing his sporty new Chevrolet coupe out of an alley at full speed.

Plans were drawn up to rob the bank in the nearby village of Daleville, hometown of Ken Trietsch's wife. On the spur of the moment the night before the bank job they held up the Bide-A-Wee Inn, a Muncie tavern, and ran into a little trouble. Later Noble Claycomb confessed that the robbers were himself, Shaw and "Dan" Dillinger. The Muncie papers dubbed him "Desperate Dan."

Whether it was with Claycomb and Shaw or perhaps Copeland and another man, Dillinger went ahead with the Daleville robbery. The lone female teller wasn't suspicious when the neatly dressed Dillinger walked in, asked a few questions and then pulled out a gun while saying, "Well, honey, this is a stickup." He then easily vaulted over the six-foot barrier in what would become his trademark method of beginning a bank robbery.

A few days later Dillinger and a second man held up the bank in the small town of Montpelier northeast of Muncie. They eluded police by throwing roofing nails on the road behind them, leaving their frustrated pursuers with flat tires. Homer Van Meter was identified as the second man. That was never proven but the use of nails was a Van Meter trademark. If it were indeed Van Meter, John was finally working with a real pro rather than a shaky group of amateurs.

By now Dillinger had attracted the attention of Matt Leach, head of the Indiana State Police. Capturing the elusive "Desperate Dan" became an obsession with Leach. Not only did he fail to do so, he was taunted by several letters sent to him by Dillinger, whose dry Hoosier sense of humor sometimes overrode common sense. While enjoying the sights at the Chicago World's Fair in the company of a girl, Dillinger handed a camera to a policeman and had him snap their picture.

The guns needed for the break were obtained and smuggled into the prison, other preparations were made and everything was set, then Dillinger got himself arrested. His desire to be with a woman from Dayton, Ohio that he had taken to the Chicago World's Fair plus the work of Pinkerton's National Detective Agency were responsible.

Among other robberies he committed during that period, John held up the bank in the small town of Bluffton, Ohio. Pinkerton's was hired to solve the case and in short order informed the Dayton police that Dillinger would be visiting a girl there and even supplied them with the make and color of the car he would be driving, a black Terraplane.

They missed him, so Pinkerton's supplied them with the name and address of the girl. Having been practically led to him by the hand, the Dayton police made the arrest. Dillinger was transferred to the jail in Lima to stand trial for the Bluffton bank job.

The prison break, the biggest in Indiana history, went off without a hitch on September 26, 1933. The ten escapees immediately split up. Those with Pierpont – they would become known as the first Dillinger gang – assembled in Indianapolis, then quickly moved to a house in Hamilton, Ohio.

The group was comprised of Harry Pierpont, John Hamilton, Charlie Makley, Russell Clark and Ed Shouse. Joining them was Harry Copeland. The latter two were destined to be booted out of the gang by Pierpont. Hamilton was often called "Red" or "Three Finger," having lost the other two as a boy when neighborhood kids would ride their sleds down a hill and see how close they could come to passing trains. The daredevil Hamilton came a bit too close.

Pierpont's first priority was to free Dillinger from the jail in Lima. To obtain some much needed money, the gang held up the bank in St. Marys, Ohio, Makley's hometown. Lima was just a short distance to the north so an evening or two later Pierpont, Makley and Clark walked into the sheriff's office

JOHN HAMILTON (This and and the two previous mug shots were in the files of the Muncie, Indiana Police Department)

while Shouse stood watch on the corner and Hamilton did the same in front of a theater just down the street.

Allen County Sheriff Jess Sarber, his wife and a deputy were in the office. When Pierpont said they were officers from the prison at Michigan City and wanted to talk to Dillinger, Sarber asked to see their credentials. Pulling a gun from his pocket, Pierpont told him, "Here's our credentials," and fired. The unfortunate sheriff died a short time later.

Studying Harry Pierpont, known to his friends as Pete, would be a psychiatrist's dream come true. During a bank robbery in Racine, Wisconsin a man and woman were taken hostage. When the woman complained that she was cold as they drove along, Pierpont took off his overcoat, wrapped it around her and asked if she was comfortable. When the man said his head was cold and asked if he could cover it with a handkerchief, Makley told him no. Pierpont took off his hat and placed it on the man's head. When Makley began cursing, Pierpont said, "Cut it out, Mac, there's a lady present."

Later, when talking with an Indianapolis reporter, Pierpont agreed that he'd be a good subject for study. After making a number of statements he said, "In the last few years of my life there's never been a day but that some incident hasn't occurred to make me hate the law. I suppose I'm what you'd call an abnormal mental case, a case for a psychiatrist. Maybe I am, but once I was normal. Place your own construction on what I've said."

After leaving Lima the gang split into two groups and headed for Chicago. Along the way those in Dillinger's car held up the police station in Auburn, Indiana and left with a submachine gun, several rifles, bulletproof vests and more than a thousand rounds of ammunition. Not long after that Pierpont walked into the police station in Peru, Indiana carrying a Thompson submachine gun. Dillinger followed holding a pistol. The three cops present watched them leave with another machine gun, shotguns, other weapons and more ammunition.

So incensed by all this was Matt Leach that he decided to split up the gang by announcing that Dillinger was the leader even though he knew it really was Pierpont. The tactic, or so he believed, would lead to a quarrel and a parting of the ways. The plan failed. Pierpont didn't care who got the credit and made the headlines while Dillinger, who saved all the clippings, grew more quiet and conservative.

And make the headlines they did. Soon the entire country was following the escapades of the Dillinger Gang. So famous were they that the gang was credited with far more bank robberies than they could possibly have committed unless they managed to be in Texas at 10 a.m. and upstate New York by noon. In reality their activities were restricted to the Midwest, the country familiar to them.

While Pierpont was the dominant figure, the gang was quite democratic. Everyone took part in planning their robberies and if someone didn't go along with the idea it was scrapped. Several of them did have girlfriends living with them but drinking was taboo. Violating that rule cost Copeland his place in the gang. Shouse was thrown out for making passes at Dillinger's girlfriend, definitely an imprudent move.

Each job was carefully planned and staged with precision, although things occasionally went wrong. There was nothing laughable to those in a bank at the sight of several neatly dressed men wearing business suits, neckties and fedoras walking in carrying submachine guns and pistols, but on one or two occasions things did turn a little humorous. The day the gang held up the bank in Greencastle, Indiana, for example.

Greencastle is a typical small Indiana county seat with a stately courthouse on the town square and business blocks facing it on four sides. The city is different than similar county seats in one respect; it is the home of DePauw University.

Catty-corner from the bank was a J.C. Penney store. John Hamilton was left outside as the guard, the "tiger" in their terminology. It was his job to see that no one left or entered the bank. Did this job frequently fall to him because of his hot temper and quickness on the trigger?

A small, elderly woman of foreign extraction was in the bank but decided to leave while Dillinger, Pierpont, Clark and Makley were at work. Hamilton reached out to stop her but she shook him off, saying, "I go to Penney's and you go to hell." The nonplussed Hamilton watched her walk away and cross the street to the department store.

Makley and Pierpont joked about the way Dillinger had vaulted over the barrier in the bank so he never did it again. He did, however, later decide to phone Matt Leach and say, "How are you, you stuttering bastard?" He continued to call Leach whenever the urge struck. And when his girlfriend said she couldn't fix his breakfast because she didn't know how to cook he said, "Start learning."

John Hamilton killed a Chicago policeman who was waiting for him in a service garage after receiving a tip that an Auburn sedan belonging to the gang was there being repaired. When Hamilton arrived, he fired first.

The gang spent the Christmas holidays at a house they had rented in Daytona Beach. While there Dillinger forced his girlfriend, Billie Frechette, to leave following an argument. He gave her $1,000 and his new car so she could return to her home in Wisconsin. When the gang decided to go to Tucson and hide out, Dillinger wanted to first try to talk her into returning. That meant passing through Chicago, where he made another of his prank calls, this one to Frank Reynolds, the cop in charge of the "Dillinger Squad."

In need of money, Dillinger and Hamilton, who had accompanied him on the trip, held up the bank in East Chicago, Indiana. Unlike the jobs organized by Pierpont, this one was poorly planned and turned sour. When cops arrived there was a gun fight and policeman Patrick O'Malley was killed. Dillinger was reported to have fired the fatal shot. He always

94

denied it. Hamilton was seriously wounded and fell, but Dillinger went back while under fire and helped him to their car. Miraculously, they made a successful escape.

Dillinger did talk Billie Frechette into traveling to Tucson with him, but soon after their arrival everything went wrong for the gang. One by one in separate places and at different times Makley, Clark, Pierpont and Dillinger were taken by surprise and captured.

By coincidence, a Tucson reporter was also from St. Marys, Ohio and Makley had known his father. During their conversation Makley said all members of his family were honest but that wasn't the life for him. "I've lived as long in forty minutes at times as my dad did in forty years." That, in just a few words, summed up the outlook of all the outlaws.

The others also had something to say. Clark contended he was going to buy a football helmet because, "Every time we get in trouble I get hit over the head."

When the governor of Arizona arrived to look over the prisoners, Pierpont said, " Well, governor, I'm sorry to see you here." He later said to the policemen who had arrested him, "There are two kinds of officers – rats and gentlemen. You fellows are gentlemen and the Indiana and Ohio cops are rats."

It was Dillinger, though, who rather accurately pointed out that, "We're exactly like you cops. You have a profession – we have a profession. Only difference is you're on the right side of the law, we're on the wrong."

John turned surly, though, and refused to leave his cell to meet the governor. His biggest concern was finding someone who would give his newly acquired puppy a good home.

Indiana, Ohio and Wisconsin all wanted possession of the gangsters and a battle for them ensued. When the fireman who had given police the original tip leading to the captures asked them to verify his story so he could collect the reward offered by *True Detective* magazine they refused, claiming they should get the money.

When Dillinger was advised to waive extradition to Indiana he grinned. "I haven't a thing to do when I get there."

He was furious and fought like a tiger when without an extradition hearing he was dragged to a small plane that would fly him to Indiana. When his leg was shackled to a seat post in the plane he said, "Hell, I don't jump out of these things."

Dillinger was taken to an "escape proof" jail in the little town of Crown Point to stand trial for the killing of the East Chicago policeman. Soon after his arrival, news photographer's gathered in the office to take pictures of him with the county prosecutor, Robert Estill. While Estill was distracted, Dillinger, the hint of a sardonic smile on his face, rested his arm on the prosecutor's shoulder. Estill's arm

appeared to be around Dillinger. The "good buddies" photo created a furor. It was said to cost Estill a shot at being governor and Indiana Governor Paul V. McNutt his chance of running for president.

On March 3, 1934 Dillinger put the capper on all his performances by escaping from the jail at Crown Point despite the unusual number of guards on hand as well as Indiana National Guardsmen. He claimed he did it with a wooden gun carved from a washboard. Obviously not one belonging to Hezzie. The police, hoping to look less like the fools that John had made of them, claimed the gun was real. No one will ever be certain, but Dillinger was photographed holding a wooden gun in one hand, a submachine gun in the other during another risky visit to Mooresville. Adding insult to injury, he made his getaway in the sheriff's car after disabling all the others in the jail's garage.

Dillinger headed for Chicago and once there quickly organized another gang with John Hamilton serving as his right hand man.   Another addition was a little, kill-crazy man named Lester Gilles. He liked to be called Big George but was better known as Baby Face Nelson.   No one ever called him that to his face, of course. The trio, accompanied by Billie Frechette, headed for St.

BABY FACE NELSON

Paul to link up with Homer Van Meter, who had been robbing banks in that area for quite some time. He brought in two more men, Eddie Green, an expert at casing banks, and Tommy Carroll, a handy man with a machine gun.

At Green's suggestion, the new gang quickly held up a bank in Sioux Falls, South Dakota. It was not the smooth type of operation organized by Harry Pierpont, at times bordering on a bad comedy, but they escaped with more than $40,000. Not, however, before the wild-eyed Nelson shot a man. The escape was aided by Van Meter's old trick of scattering roofing nails behind the getaway car.

Dillinger used much of his share to pay lawyers for Pierpont's trial in Lima. He was convicted, with the help of damning testimony from former colleague Ed Shouse, and he and Makley were sentenced to death. Clark was handed a life sentence. When the prosecutor accused Pierpont of getting $300,000 from bank robberies he denied it, then caused laughter in the courtroom by saying, "Well, at least if I did I'm not like some bank robbers – I didn't get myself elected president of the bank first."

Pierpont and Makley later attempted to break out of the Ohio State Penitentiary in Columbus. Makley was killed and Pierpont wounded. Nursed back to health, he then was put to death in the electric chair.

Dillinger was wounded in a shootout at his apartment in St. Paul, but once again the police botched up the job and he escaped. Of all the places on earth he would be expected to avoid, Mooresville topped the list and yet that's where he went to recuperate.

Back in action, he and Van Meter held up another police station, this one in Warsaw, Indiana. Then they held up the bank in Mason City, Iowa in what amounted to another fiasco. During the course of some serious gunplay, Dillinger, Hamilton and Van Meter were wounded, none seriously. Nelson again shot a bystander. Again roofing nails came into play but Dillinger had to scold Baby Face for scattering them under their own car.

In need of a rest, the gang decided a good place for it would be the Little Bohemia Lodge in the northern reaches of Wisconsin.

For several days Dillinger, Hamilton, Nelson, Van Meter and Carroll relaxed, playing cards and taking a little target practice. But people, including the owner of the lodge and his wife, were suspicious and managed to tip off the FBI. What followed was another FBI fiasco.

Led by Melvin Purvis, agents positioned themselves outside the lodge in the dark of night. Three customers who lived nearby left the lodge and the FBI opened fire, killing one of them and severally wounding the other two. A story supplied to a website by the FBI makes no mention of that.

Alerted by the gun shots, four of the gangsters who had been playing cards in the lodge returned the fire. So did Baby Face Nelson from a nearby cabin. With the agents milling around in front of the lodge, four of the gang jumped out of a second story window at the back, landing in a snow bank that cushioned their fall. They escaped by running to the right along the lakeshore. Nelson did the same by running to the left. At a house a short distance away, Nelson killed an FBI agent and severely wounded a second.

In three separate cars, all five members of the gang escaped the area. Meanwhile the FBI agents continued firing at the lodge, eventually engulfing it with teargas. Three young women came stumbling out, tears streaming down their faces. And so ended the "battle" at the Little Bohemia lodge.

The nation was appalled by the incompetent performance of the FBI in not only failing to capture the men they were after but shooting innocent parties in the process. Humorist Will Rogers wrote, "Well, they had Dillinger surrounded and was all ready to shoot him when he come out, but another bunch of folks come out ahead, so they just shot them instead. Dillinger is going to accidentally get with some innocent bystanders sometime, then he will get shot."

Reading the accounts of the events, Dillinger must have been smiling. However, while driving south from Little Bohemia a day or so later the stolen car in which

AN AMUSED JOHNNIE

Dillinger, Hamilton and Van Meter were riding was spotted and Hamilton was shot in the back. Nearly a week of trying to find a doctor willing to treat him proved fruitless and he died. He was buried in a gravel pit after having lye poured on his hands and face to prevent his body from being identified. Dillinger handled the job himself, saying, "I hate to do this, Red, but I know you'd do the same to me."

The heat was really on by the time Van Meter and Dillinger arrived in Chicago. They didn't make it easy on themselves by abandoning a bloodstained Ford on a city street. Every cop in the country was on the lookout for it. They managed to hide out, though, and with the help of his lawyer, Dillinger arranged to have plastic surgery. Van Meter did the same. The work

99

did little to alter their features. Even so, Dillinger paid a visit to his Indiana home at Mooresville and spent another day at the World's Fair in Chicago.

In the meantime, Tommy Carroll was killed in a shootout with police. Then Van Meter suffered a head wound when he, Dillinger, Nelson and a couple of unidentified men held up a bank in South Bend. A policeman was killed in the shootout that followed. The robbery netted the gang only $20,000. The take disappointed Dillinger, who was hoping to accumulate enough money to travel to Mexico.

For a short time, though, he managed to live the quiet life of an ordinary citizen in Chicago, doing such things as attending a Cubs baseball game at Wrigley Field. He also was dating a woman named Polly Hamilton – no relation to John. An older woman, Anna Sage, became his friend and came to know his true identity. Dillinger was confident she would not betray him, but she did.

The events of the hot July night when he took the two women to the Biograph Theater are well known. In a hail of gunfire as they left the theater, Dillinger at last was killed. In the process two female bystanders

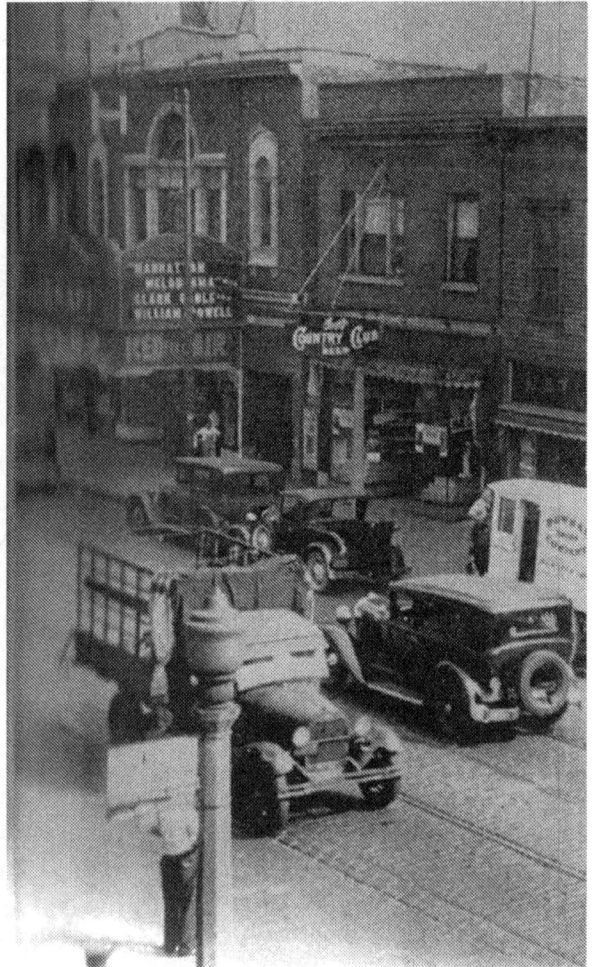

were wounded. Ironically, the last movie seen by Dillinger was *Manhattan Melodrama* in which Clark Gable played the role of a criminal sentenced to death, thanks to the work of his friend, Prosecutor William Powell.

But was it really Dillinger who died or a small-time criminal set up to take the fall? All the evidence indicates it was indeed John Dillinger, yet there have always been doubters. The color of the eyes were wrong and the coroner's explanation that being in the sun could have caused the change was weak at best. The first photo taken of the body lying on a slab in the morgue showed he was wearing a ring. Dillinger never wore jewelry because it was identifiable. In subsequent pictures the ring was gone. Despite stories to the contrary, it seems almost certain that the body buried at Crown Hill Cemetery in Indianapolis was Dillinger's.

A month after Dillinger's death, Homer Van Meter would die in another gun battle with police in St. Paul. Four months after the fateful night at the Biograph, Baby Face Nelson was killed in yet another shootout, but not before he killed two more FBI agents, giving him a total of three to his credit.

And so ended the Dillinger era. It had lasted a mere thirteen months but placed his name among the leading figures in crime. Just another unknown criminal when it began, he came to be a legend in his own time and actually grew to become the man it had made him out to be.

Other flamboyant outlaws became famous, or infamous, during the years of the Great Depression. Pretty Boy Floyd, Ma Barker and her sons Dock and Fred, Alvin Karpis, Bonnie Parker and Clyde Barrow, their names will live on so long as people are intrigued by crime and criminals. Those desperadoes of the 1930s were unique, unlike any before or after. They bore no resemblance to the big city gangster spawned by Prohibition. They robbed banks, escaped in fast cars, shot it out with the police whenever the need arose. And sooner or later they died in a blaze of gunfire.

Why were so many people fascinated by their exploits. Certainly not for the reason given in a typically self-serving FBI text which claims, "During the 1930s Depression, many Americans, nearly helpless against forces they didn't understand, made heroes of outlaws who took what they wanted at gunpoint."

Forces they didn't understand? Oh, they understood perfectly. They understood the bank failures that cost so many their life savings. They understood the bank foreclosures that cost a countless number their homes and farms. When a group of neatly dressed outlaws walked into a bank and left with large sums of money, people indeed understood. They understood it was payback for what had been done to so many of them and they found it deeply satisfying.

And while the exploits of the outlaws were making headlines that often provided a laugh, Americans found a very different reason to laugh on Saturday night when they tuned into the National Barn Dance on radio.

MOVING ON TO HOLLYWOOD

What a roller coaster ride the decade of the 1930s had been for Hezzie, Ken and Gabe. The breakup of the Buzzington band and the end of touring on vaudeville, menial jobs at Montgomery Ward, one-night stands resulting from their unpaid show on WOWO, moving on to Chicago and the National Barn Dance, recording dozens of phonograph records and finally an appearance in a Hollywood movie.

There would be little in the way of a downside for the boys during the 1940s and early 1950s. Recording dates would fall off, though, after big years in 1940 and '41. In 1942 only three Hot Shot records were released and none at all during 1943.

This was because of an action by American Federation of Musicians President James C. Petrillo. In a move aimed at getting the recording companies to pay higher royalties he ruled that union members could not make records. The Hot Shots and the big bands were among those who paid a severe price because non-union artists and vocal groups *did* record during what amounted to a strike lasting nearly two years. Some critics have credited Petrillo with the demise of the Big Band Era.

While unable to make records, the Hot Shots returned to Hollywood to film *Hoosier Holiday* in 1943 and then two more movies in 1944, including *The National Barn Dance*.

GIL TAYLOR SITS IN FRONT OF THE BOYS

A change in personnel was necessary when in 1943 Frank Kettering was drafted for service in World War II. Near the end of the year he was replaced as bass player by Gil Taylor, a handsome native of Alabama known for his fine singing voice.

The Hot Shots continued to appear on the National Barn Dance as well as doing their own radio show for Alka-Seltzer and a Servicemen's Radio Party every Wednesday night. In 1944 they took time out to do a USO tour that led them to North Africa and Italy. Ken, who had constructed Hezzie's washboard, built a new, lightweight model for the trip. Gabe said that wherever they performed for the GIs their first request was always for *Back Home Again in Indiana.* As noted in the clipping on a following page, they always offered, once they were back in the States, to send postcards to the family of any GI who signed a request. They counted them during the trip home and had more than 10,000 cards to prepare and mail. No matter where they traveled, the boys never forgot to promote and never lost touch with their fans.

When they resumed recording it was on the Decca label. Nine sides were released in 1944 and six the following year, as well as two V-Discs for the military. After that it was downhill with only thirteen sides released during the next dozen or more years, although later on they made some Long Play records.

Three more of their songs did make the charts, one in 1944 and two in 1946. The first was *She Broke My Heart In Three Places*, which also appeared on a soundie. In 1946 *Someday (You'll Want Me To Want You)* made both the Pop Music and the Country Music charts. The latter wasn't yet in existence when the earlier Hot Shot hits were recorded.

On an audio tape he made for me, Gabe Ward told this story about *Someday.* "Dave Kapp, who was head of Decca's country music division at the time, flew out from New York to Chicago and said he had this song that was going to be a big hit and asked if any of us could sing it. I sang two bars and he said, 'No, you can't do it.' I said, 'I didn't think so.' So Gil Taylor said, 'Let me see that.' He looked it over, then started singing and Kapp said, 'That's it! Just the right southern touch.' So we made the record and it sold 600,000 copies, but a few years later Vaughn Monroe did it and sold a million.

Listen to *Someday* on tape or CD and the singer is a man, Gil Taylor. So why do some sources say it was Sally Foster? Even Joel Whitburn's *Pop Memories 1890-1954*, the definitive source for hit records, claims it was Sally, also a National Barn Dance performer. Gabe's story seems to settle the matter.

Another hit recording for the Hot Shots, their last to make the charts, was also released in 1946. Their *Sioux City Sue* was just one of many versions of the hugely popular song. Best known of them was Bing Crosby's recording. The boys imported Dick "Two-Ton" Baker, a popular Chicago radio personality, to do the singing (see Chapter 17). It proved to be Baker's biggest hit but he didn't get top billing on the label. That went to the Hoosier Hot Shots.

The boys appeared in four movies in 1945, five the following year and three in 1947. With their focus shifted from recordings and radio shows to movies, they were spending more and more time in Hollywood. The commuting between Chicago and Hollywood proved to be too time consuming, too expensive and just too much of a hassle in general. It was time, they decided, to settle in permanently on the West Coast.

GABE TITLED THIS "A NEW SUIT, AN OLD CLARINET"

The move was made in July of 1946. Prior to that, however, they had to buy new houses, sell those back in Chicago and make arrangements for continuing to do their shows on radio.

Ken and Hezzie found houses in North Hollywood. Gil and his family lived for a time in a trailer at a court in Burbank inhabited by movie people. But Gabe, who said he turned a

105

profit on the sale of his home in Chicago, couldn't find a house with four bedrooms in Hollywood so he, Marguerite and their three children settled into one he bought in Encino. Their neighbors, Gabe said, included Clark Gable, Mary Astor, Alice Faye and Phil Harris, Teresa Wright, Al Jolson and Ruby Keeler and old WLS radio stars Fibber McGee and Molly.

The photo and stories above are poor copies but they manage to provide a few details of the move. Dave Ward is Gabe, of course. The logistics of a seven-vehicle caravan traveling from Chicago to the west coast are beyond imagining. Fortunately they had houses awaiting their arrival.

So that left the problem of doing their radio shows. "It was a hectic time," said Gabe and it would be difficult to argue with that statement. It was their old friend Alka-Seltzer that came to the rescue by allowing them to record on the coast. The programs were then piped back to Chicago.

So for the following four years they were kept busy doing radio shows and making movies, many of them westerns starring a handsome young singing cowboy named Ken Curtis.

'LONE STAR MOONLIGHT' Gleams Brightly for Cornfed Boxoffice

Clark And Nazarro Ride Bucolic Tuner To Market; Hoosier Hotshots Swell

"LONE STAR MOONLIGHT"
(Columbia)

OKAY

80%

Directed by Ray Nazarro. Producer: Colbert Clark. Screenplay by Louise Rousseau. Original story by Louise Rousseau. Ande Lamb. Director of Photography: George F. Keller. Film editor: Paul Borofsky. Art direction: Charles Clague. Set decorator: William Kiernan. Musical director: Paul Mertz. Caught at Opening at Glen City Theatre, Santa Paula, Calif., Jan. 5, 1947. Release date, December 12, 1946. Running time, 67 minutes.

With the skill born of practised success, Columbia's latest A-Burner under the hand of Colbert Clark and with Ray Nazarro driving down box-office road at the steering wheel, "Lone Star Moonlight," the umpteenth hit of the wide open spaces, is just about the best of the lot. Since the Hoosier Hotshots graduated to top billing in the casts and the stories are more than ever slanted toward them, they are more nonsensical fun than ever.

Curt Norton, a returning GI who formerly owned the local radio station and is now trying to get a television license, finds that his father, Amos Norton, has let the station run down during his absence. Curt and the Hoosier Hotshots, partners in the radio station, run into trouble with Eddie Jackson, who came to town while Curt was at war and opened a rival station. Jackson is also trying to get a television license and is making advances to Curt's girl, Jean White, daughter of Amos' deadly enemy for the past twenty years. Things look pretty bad for Curt, more so when he finds out that the money he had been sending to his father for upkeep of the station has been badly invested. Curt has no money, no radio station. Jean comes up with an idea for a big auction, with dancing and entertainment. A raft of singers and musicians, including Curt and Jean, are lined up for the event. Jackson sets about to throw a monkey wrench into the affair. He hires a Hollywood actress, Mimi, to pretend she is a French girl whom Curt married while overseas. She confronts Curt at a moment when Jean and a lot of witnesses are with him, and makes a big scene. Curt, flabbergasted, tries to deny the marriage but everybody believes the worst. Jean is heartbroken and walks away. Curt decides to hold the auction anyway.

Meanwhile, Mimi, who has been living with Jean, has a change of heart and confesses. Jean immediately rushes to Curt and there's a reconciliation. Curt goes after Jackson and gives him a sound thrashing. The auction and entertainment are successful. Curt gets the girl, money for the radio station

The Cast of Characters
with
THE HOOSIER HOTSHOTS
(Hezzie, Ken, Gil and Gabe)

Curt Norton	Ken CURTIS
Jean White	Joan BARTON
Amos Norton	Guy KIBBEE
Eddie Jackson	Robert STEVENS
Mimi	Claudia DRAKE

The Smart Set
Merle Travis Trio
Judy Clark and Her Rhythm Cowgirls
and

Thaddeus White	Arthur Loft
Sheriff	Vernon Dent
Mahoney	Sam Flint

and the television license.

This is the idea concocted by Louise Rousseau and Ande Lamb that comes off much more brightly than it reads in Miss Rousseau's often devastating screenplay, and it is a sturdy oak on which these bucolic musical talents cling. Ken Curtis sings better and gets more handsome each time. The Hotshots are easy favorites in their market. Joan Barton is a very fresh and lovely country heroine and Claudia Drake gives her vamp role some sultry class. Guy Kibbee is a riot in his standby characterization and the late Arthur Loft gets some good scenes for himself. Judy Clark is but terrific!

The songs are six and they are "It's Great To Be Back," "Catalogue Cowboy," "Go West, Young Lady," "That's What Interests Me," "When Johnny Brings Lelani Home," and the title tune, "Lone Star Moonlight," and the hummiest of the crop. Their use makes a good credit for Paul Mertz.

—J. H.

Hotshots Sign For 16
The Hoosier Hotshots yesterday inked a new pact with Columbia for four action musicals a year for four years under the Colbert Clark unit. Present contract has 18 months to run.

Hwd Rptr 1/21/47

Hoosier Hot Shots Get New Col Pact
With 18 months still to go on their old pact, Hoosier Hot Shots have been inked by Columbia to new four-year deal calling for four pictures a year during that period. They will continue starring in musical Westerns produced for Gower street studio by Colbert Clark.

Variety 1/22/47

"The start of our big money times — 1945-1954"

gabe

If the boys had any notions that making movies would be a piece of cake, they soon learned otherwise. In his *Hollywood Showdown* newspaper gossip column, Evans Plummer wrote this about the filming of *In Old Monterey,* the first movie made by the Hot Shots:

"HOLLYWOOD – If you ask Gabe Ward and his fellow Hoosier Hot Shots – Hezzie, Ken and Frank – of "Uncle Ezra" and "National Barn Dance" fame, who were here for their first time to appear in Gene Autry's new Republic picture "In Old Monterey," this town isn't half as bad as it's cracked up to be. "We thought Hollywood was just a big pot of glamour that boiled the life out of people in a few short years," he told your reporter, "but were we ever wrong! Our first studio call was for 4:30 a.m. and we sure went to bed at nine o'clock that night without coaxing. Never saw such hard-working people anywhere, not even back home in Indiana. Everybody awake and working at sun-up to make full use of the daylight. Then look at clean-cut, friendly Gene Autry, whom we knew at WLS. Why, say, he hasn't changed a bit. Three weeks here has taught us that Hollywood glamour is just a parlor name for hard work."

So when the Hot Shots packed up and moved to the coast they knew what to expect. Long hours and hard work were no strangers to them, of course, so movie-making was just different, that's all. And they still had other obligations. While most members of a cast might be finished for the day when the filming ended, the boys had radio shows to think about. As Gabe pointed out on the previous page, these were their big money times – but they earned every cent they made.

ITALIANS FORGET OPERA; GO FOR HOT SHOTS' CORN

'West Side' Tune Makes Hit with GIs

BY LARRY WOLTERS

Toscanini doesn't know it yet, but his favorite opera house—La Scala in Milan, Italy—was recently plastered with billboards announcing the coming of the Hoosier Hot Shots to entertain GIs.

A lank young Yank looked over the posters and remarked to a buddy: "Say, I wonder if those guys speak English?"

What they had to say with their outlandish collection of Barn Dance instruments was understood not only by the GIs but by Italian musicians. The Hot Shots got back last week and reported that the Italians practically forgot "Celeste, Aida" and took up "Don't Fence Me In" as a substitute.

Join Italian Jammers

The "cultured corn" of the Hot Shots was a revelation to the Milanese, Neapolitans, and Romans. Italian music makers invited the Hot Shots to sit in on the Mediterranean equivalent of the jam session. If post-war Italian music brings forth a crop of hybrid "corn," the Hot Shots will be responsible.

The Italians went into raptures over "Il Lava Bordo," that is to say the washboard. Hezzie Trietsch, the washboard maestro, inspired more pushing, yelling and jamming than Van Johnson and Frank Sinatra at a bobby-soxers' convention. The fans pursued them to their hotels and yelled for autographs.

Ken Trietsch, who doubles as manager of the outfit and "gittar man," had whipped up a special light weight stainless steel washboard in his home workshop before the boys went overseas. The boys were afraid that salt water spray might ruin their old stand-by, a galvanized job. They turned down all offers for the washboard, both from musicians, and women who wanted it for rubbing the long underwear.

Cheer Chicago Tune

Chicagoans raised the rafters every time the Hot Shots swung into their opening number, "The West Side of Chicago," a rootin'-tootin' affair replete with sound effects. The tune, written by Jack Frost of the National Barn Dance staff, is featured in their new movie, "Rockin' in the Rockies."

Recording companies put thumbs down when the Hot Shots wanted to add it to their list of discs, fearing that sensitive Chicagoans might not like some of the noisome references to their home town. But Chicagoans in Italy gave it rousing approval.

Ken and Hezzie, Gabe Ward, clarinetist, and Gil Taylor, who handles the bass, have something more to do than get ready for the 12th anniversary of the Barn Dance [and their own] on Sept. 29.

While abroad they offered to send postcard messages to the families and friends of every American service man who put in a request. At each show service men had an opportunity to sign up. On the way home the Hot Shots counted the names. The list runs a little over 10,000!

Dick - My pen-pal list is not that big . — Lots o' work — Gabeelo

109

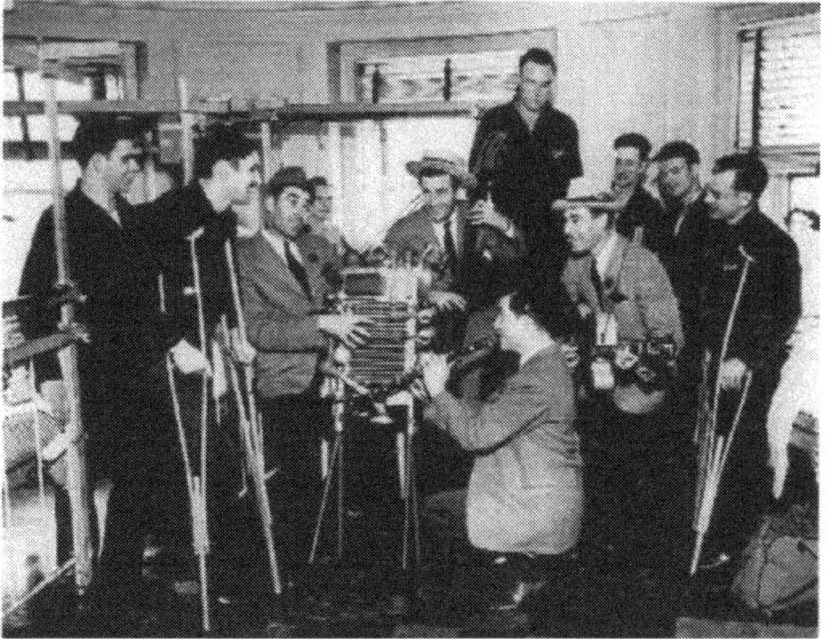

Wherever they went during their USO tour in North Africa and Europe the Hot Shots made a point of visiting as many Army hospitals such as the one above as possible. They did the same at both military and civilian hospitals and extended care facilities in the States. While there was no monetary payoff for this, at least not immediately, the return in good will was immeasurable. That was not their reason for paying such visits, however, it was just something they enjoyed doing. Their early visits to such places, as Gabe said, had taught them about Lonely Street.

WINDING DOWN

The last movie made by the Hot Shots was released early in 1950. They had ended their long association with the National Barn Dance in 1947, but during 1950 and 1951 they had their own radio show on the Mutual network. They also kept busy with personal appearances, many of them lengthy engagements in Las Vegas. So for a few years the money continued to roll in and then life began to slow down for the boys.

While their movies were playing they had traveled throughout the country by train doing live performances to accompany the films. As the 1950s advanced, though, they were ready to cut back on their work load. Ken, Hezzie and Gabe had invested their earnings wisely so they could afford a more leisurely routine while still keeping the group together.

Gil, who had always received a smaller cut of the earning because of being a late arrival, left the group in the late 1950s when their activities were scaled back. After that he earned a living selling and repairing electronic equipment. On weekends and some nights he kept his hand in the music business by playing with various groups.

Even though they weren't as busy as they had been in the past, Ken, Gabe and Hezzie weren't ready to disband the Hot Shots so they added a new man, Nate Harrison. He had grown up in Las Vegas, a far cry indeed from the flatlands of Indiana. Nate was a veteran musician, having played professionally since the time the Hot Shots were getting started in the 1930s. During World War II he was a member of Army bands and prior to that had been in a Dollar Line band that played on ocean liners and for a time backed up Bing Crosby vocals on guitar. He replaced Gil on string bass with the Hot Shots and also filled in on guitar.

In 1960 Keith Milheim joined the act. Ironically, he had spent his boyhood days in Van Wert, Ohio, the little town not far from Fort Wayne where the Hot Shots had worked for a time at Montgomery Ward. He also had served in World War

II and after being discharged joined the Don Ragon band. Keith had a fine singing voice and was a skilled whistler as well as a drummer so those were the talents he brought to the Hot Shots. By then the boys were performing only when it suited them so Keith spent his days working as a tree trimmer.

Hezzie also went into business, opening a pawn shop. At last report it is still in operation.

KEN DONNED A TOP HAT FOR THIS PHOTO OF THE FINAL GROUP OF HOT SHOTS – HEZZIE, NATE, KEN, GABE AND KEITH

Gabe said they had a standard opening and closing routine for shows during the late years. Before the program got under way Hezzie, after asking if anyone in the audience had seen their movies and finding that many had, would say, "Looks like we have some old ones out there." Ken would reply, "That's okay, we have some old ones up here." Vintage Hoosier Hot Shot humor, dry as the Indiana flatlands during a July with little rain.

At the end of the show Hezzie would tell a few unsophisticated jokes. Here's a word-for-word example taken from the recording of one live performance:

"There was a guy leadin' a little bitty ole yellow dog down the street and here come a guy towards him leadin' a great big ole vicious looking dog. The guy almost stepped on the little one and the guy with the big dog said be awful careful, don't let that little dog get close to this big dog because this big dog is vicious, he's liable to hurt that little dog. 'Bout that time the little dog reached over and bit the big dog's leg off. The guy said what in the world kind of a dog have you got there? He said well before we cut his tail and snout off and painted him yellow he was an alligator."

It was funnier when Hezzie's high-pitched laughter could be heard. He went on:

"Ya know last summer on my vacation I went down to the southern part of Arkansas to visit a friend of mine. He lived out in the country. I drove up to the farm house, got out of the car, went up on the front porch. I noticed there was fish scales all over the front porch. I went into the house, there was fish scales all over the house. I said hey Luke I see you been goin' fishing. He says no, why? I said well there's fish scales every-where. He says heck, man, those are toenails. We had a dance here last night."

Hezzie's laughter helped that one, too. He continued:

"There was a guy drivin' a truck up over the mountain pass the other day and he'd go about a hundred feet or a hundred-fifty feet or so and he'd stop, stop the truck, get out of the truck, had a great big ole club, he'd start a beatin' on the side of the truck. He went clear around the truck beatin' on the side of it with this great big ole club and get back in the truck, he'd drive a hundred feet or so, stop, get out and with the big ole club he'd start beatin' on the side of the truck. He kept this up, finally a cop pulled him over and he says, I see you stop every little bit and start beatin' on the side of that truck. What's the big idea? He says, officer, this is a one ton truck and I've got two tons o' canaries in there and I gotta keep half o' them flyin'."

With Hezzie's crazy laugh the routine really was funny. He then would say they had been a wonderful audience and how much the boys had enjoyed visiting with them. Hezzie would invite them to pay a return visit, explaining the route to follow as quoted earlier:

You simply turn to the right at the crossroads,
And then turn left at the little red barn,
Turn down the lane of memories,
Gaze at the stars that used to be,
Then go straight down the pathway of childhood,
Where the red leaves of dreams tumble down.
Though you arrive, just in imagination,
We'll all greet you at the station,
In our town – everyone's home town.
That's it.

When Hezzie's final word was spoken all the boys would immediately begin a rousing finale.

The Hot Shots made a couple of Long Play records during the sixties. Some of the songs were their old standards but they also included some new numbers. In most cases the "new" songs were old familiar standbys being played for the first time by the Hot Shots. By then the pop music scene was dominated by rock 'n' roll and little if any of that was adaptable to their routine.

The boys stayed together and kept playing right through 1979. Only occasionally, of course. It wasn't until Hezzie died of cancer in April of 1980 that the Hoosier Hot Shots ceased to exist. Even after that Ken released a few items and Gabe continued to perform, sometimes as a solo but usually with a group he had gathered together.

"When I had a gig I'd pick some back-up men," he said. "I made the most money of my life but had to give it up because of Marge's illness."

Gabe was troubled when he heard that Ken had to give up driving and could no longer play golf. That had been a favorite pastime for the boys once their hectic schedule allowed for it. They often arranged to give evening performances at a country club for little if anything more than being able to play a round of golf during the afternoon. And, of course, having an opportunity to meet new people and do some socializing, They never lost their love for that.

It's doubtful that Gabe Ward was ever truly mad at anyone during his entire life. Annoyed at times, of course. Undoubtedly disappointed with someone on occasion. But really mad – he didn't seem to have that ability in his makeup. The closest I heard him come to it was on a tape. His words, which follow, seem to express disappointment rather than anger with his friend of six decades:

"Kenny, our guitar player, you know Ken Trietsch from Muncie, Hezzie's brother, he was a devout Mormon and, ah, and I went down there to settle with him after we disbanded after Hezzie died. To settle with him about a lot of our sheet music which we'd all shared equally in as far as cost and what-not was concerned. And I especially was busy with the sheet music because I had to teach Hezzie the melodies, you know, to do on his whistle and different things. I went down there and I discovered, I was absolutely amazed he had given his guitar and his tuba and bass horn and all the music and everything he'd given to the Mormon Church. They sent a truck over to Studio City and sent it all over to Provo, Utah and so that's where all my music went. So what am I gonna do? I can't, I'm not going to sue the church. I can't sue the church over Ice House Lizzie or somethin'. Oh, well, that's a little anecdote."

Gabe laughed as he said he couldn't sue the church, yet the hurt was apparent. He was still performing on his own so the sheet music would have been invaluable to him. Apparently it was merely a thoughtless act on Ken's part. Gabe didn't let it bother him for long. After Ken's wife died, Gabe wrote, "I went to sit with him."

In an interview for a newspaper story Gabe said the Hot Shots never suffered from internal friction or petty jealousies. Harmony ruled from the beginning until their final performance.

In the same interview he said, "Anybody in radio or on records was a freak in one respect: people always wondered what you looked like so they'd pack the place wherever you played. Sometimes we'd put on four or five shows a day, each about fifty minutes long, just so everybody got a chance to see us. We'd sell our songbooks, shake hands, give autographs and, a little later, sold a bunch of records that way."

Ken Trietsch's last letter to Gabe was dated July 17, 1987, two months to the day before Ken died. It came as a severe blow to Gabe, yet just as he always did he managed to remember the good times and think ahead to renewing them in this brief but heartfelt eulogy:
"My partner since vaudeville (1923-29),
 Montgomery Ward Stores (1929-32),
WOWO Fort Wayne radio (1932-33),
Chicago radio on NBC (1933-47),
Hollywood movies (1939-50),
World-wide bookings (1950-80).
Now God has a better idea 'n' I'm glad He knows best.
I was honored to be *Second Slide Whistle* and now I'll be pleased to join those in 'Washboard Heaven.'
END OF PARTNERSHIP."

Gabe and Marguerite spent their final years in Oregon so they could be close to their two sons. His beloved Marguerite, his partner since 1928 died on February 2, 1991. WOWO in Fort Wayne aired a memorial program in her honor. Gabe went on selling tapes and writing letters until his own death eleven months later – January 14, 1992. A single sentence in a long letter seemed to sum up how this most optimistic of men felt deep inside: "A type of loneliness exists."

Despite everything, Gabe managed to retain much of his optimism. In a letter written to me two days before his death he spoke of keeping busy filling orders and doing other things. "Busy, busy has a payoff," he wrote, and I'm sure he wasn't referring to money alone. Insight into the makeup of this most unusual and wonderful man can be found in an announcement of his arrival at their final home in Oregon. Read it on the next page and you won't find a single word about his days as a celebrity. Boasting was one characteristic he did not possess.

TRYING TO BEE YOUR BEST SELF
" INVOLVEMENT "

Hello Woodburn,

My name is Gabe. I'm 82 yrs. old and supposedly retired. Government and Insurance folks keep track of my financial standing. Marguerite, my wife of 58 yrs., knows more about me than they do. I believe I know more about me than she does - well almost anyway!

Arriving in Woodburn last August I at once saw plenty of things to become concerned about and began getting acquainted. Fortunately folks, both "oldies" and "youngies", are wonderful!!

Since I grew up in Indiana, spent 15 yrs. in Chicago, and 25 yrs. in Hollywood. During this time I found involvement to be the key to happiness.

Involvement in family, 14 grandchildren. Involvement in local affairs, listening to others. Contributing time and energy helping others get involved.

The secret to happiness is involvement. It's hard to get into better company than that of people working. To kill time is to murder it.

At RSVP a LITTLE INVOLVEMENT means a BIG RESULT!

Bye now,

Gabe Ward, RSVP Volunteer

BEE A BUSY BEE
BEECOME INVOLVED!

HOOSIER HOT SHOTS
Discs
5 Mins.
ALKA-SELTZER
Daily, 8:40 a. m.
WGY, Schenectady
(*Wade*)

These briefies, heard at 8:40 a. m., should contribute their share in pushing up sales charts on Alka-Seltzer. Hoosier Hot Shots, male song-instrumental group who work with Pat Barrett et al. on National Barn Dance, zip through two numbers; remainder of time is devoted to plugging.

Hot Shots are hardly for the sophisticates or rug cutters, being on the cobby side. However, they do their stuff well. One spot is for a song, with instrumental background, while the other is for ensemble playing. Second of spiels is repetitious, but on platters, advertising restraint is rare.

Station announcer, fore and aft, mentions Hot Shots as part of A-S Barn Dance. *Jaco.*

118

COLUMNS FEATURING GABE WARD AND THE HOT SHOTS

In the Press of things

By DICK STODGHILL

A letter from Ol' Gabe can make reader feel better about the world

FROM THE MUNCIE (Indiana) EVENING PRESS
Much of the material is found in the text of this book
August 16, 1983

"Ol' Gabe can't stop the music."

That's how Gabe Ward, the old Hoosier Hot Shot, headed his latest letter. I have never met or corresponded with a man of such amazing optimism or one so completely unspoiled by success. A letter from Gabe never fails to make me feel a little better about the world. Maybe they have the same effect on others so here is the most recent:

Dear Friend Dick,

Here in the middle of a long hot summer and my mail is becoming bigger 'n' more important all the time! "In the Press of Things" cooked up quite a stir and gave me some very interesting vistas about the music "biz" and also about folks' aches 'n' pains and how they are handling such things.

I'm answering every letter individually and it's a rewarding experience to be on a "one and one" basis with so many good people. To me the written word is more to be treasured than a Mona Lisa or other painting.

I've written to parents of servicemen when the men couldn't spell or write. The Hoosier Hot Shots and a Chicago office answered over 10,000 soldier boys' requests that we contact their parents. We brought those names home from Italy, Austria, and North Africa when we "cut loose" during Special Services shows, Those 1942-44 contacts created a spin-off and deluged the Miles Laboratories with Hot Shot mail. We were renewed by them at a 20 percent salary increase for several years coast to coast. An incredible success story about country boys from Indiana.

I figure if I keep on playing my clarinet and writing to people I won't know any strangers and will "never get too old." Hopefully, my Hoosier childhood and roots will not be washed away by "adulthood."

As ever, Gabe

Gabe, well past 80 now, spends about 20 hours a week at his California home transferring 78 r.p.m. records to tape. After his address was printed here he sold about 40 records to Press readers. He's a remarkable man.

October 20. 1983

Remember when the smell of burning leaves was as much a part of autumn as orange pumpkins and brown corn stalks? In some small Indiana towns it still is, but in Muncie it is all but forgotten.

The memory of that fine aroma was stirred by a letter from Gabe Ward. The old Hoosier Hot Shot now lives in California where, from what I can gather, they don't burn many leaves.

Ol' Gabe isn't a complaining man, but he came up with one. He and his wife Marguerite couldn't exchange cards on their 55th anniversary because no one bothers to print them for that

120

particular occasion. Gabe said, "What's the world coming to? Ha!"

He has been busy, though. He recently recruited a bass player from Lawrence Welk's 80th birthday party band and a guitar player from the public schools in Encinitas, then "did a gig for a hundred folks. It seemed to go very well but there was no advance promotion. Folks said, 'If I'd known I would have brought my mother.' An old story!"

Here is a quiz, but you will flunk it unless you either have a long memory or are a student of country music. Gabe enclosed an old National Barn Dance ad from 1934 naming some of the performers who could be heard every Saturday night on 24 radio stations coast to coast. Give yourself a point for every one of the following you have heard of, two points if you have actually listened to them perform:

Cumberland Ridge Runners, Linda Parker, Skyland Scotty, Maple City Four, Spareribs, Tom and Don, Lulu Belle, Hoosier Hot Shots, Uncle Ezra, Georgie Goebel, Louise Massey and the Westerners.

My score was 12, but I may have cheated a little.

May 28, 1984

You won't have to go far in July if you want to hear Gabe Ward, the old Hoosier Hot Shot, perform such Hoosier Favorites as "Back Home Again In Indiana" and "I Wish That I Was Back In Indiana." Gabe wrote that last one himself.

In his latest letter Gabe told of how he teamed up with the Trietsch brothers, Ken and Hezzie, when they were playing in the Muncie Products Band. They had been waiting for booking agents in Indianapolis and Chicago to arrange dates, but decided to strike out on their own when the agents began calling — and reversing the charges — to tell them, "Sorry, theater's closed, no money." So they went on WOWO and were instant hits with such songs as "Meet Me Tonight In the Cowshed" and "Since We Put a Radio Out In the Henhouse." Gabe, always a writer, sent a postcard to everyone who mailed a request or thank you letter to the Hoosier Hot Shots.

121

July 9, 1984

Muncie and Delaware County were well-represented Saturday at Battle Ground when fans of Gabe Ward and lovers of country and folk music gathered at Tippecanoe Battlefield Park. Others drove there Sunday for a second concert featuring stars of the old WLS Barn Dance.

We would liked to have stayed over, but had to get home if this column was to be written Sunday. Then, when it was time to sit down and begin, my mind staged a spirited but futile revolt. "Hold on, fella," it protested, "after soaking up material from eight in the morning until 2 a.m., I deserve a respite."

"Forget it," I replied. "Look at the nose – it didn't stop sneezing until 4 a.m., but do you hear it complaining?".

"I know, it kept me awake in the process. And that's all it had to do, but now you want me to keep running to the cells and pulling out memories. Not only that, you'll be at it the rest of the week. I know you, you'll want the stuff on that good place to eat, all those people we met, the park, even that about the license plates and how booze got its name. And Alexandria's old slogan, don't forget that, and Hezzie playing forward for the team at Cowan High."

"All right, all right. For now all I need is the file on the Wards, Gabe and Marguerite."

So it was delivered, along with a few weary sighs, and here it is:

Ol' Gabe, who left this area more than half a century ago to gain fame as one of the three Hoosier Hot Shots (the others were Ken and Hezzie Trietsch), was in rare form Saturday night, even though he didn't go on stage until 10:15. The Wards arrived from California by plane Friday night and we got together with them at the park the next afternoon.

Jackie and Marguerite hit it off right away. The two of them sat whispering and giggling, which was very distracting because Gabe and I were discussing serious matters such as how he would teach Hezzie the arrangements for new Hot Shot numbers. I even held his clarinet and was thinking about running off a riff or two, but then there was more giggling so what might have been a great moment in music never came to pass.

Marguerite is from North Baltimore, a little Ohio town near Findlay. "I'm from Findlay," she said, but then when I **GABE SHOWS DICK HIS CLARINET** told her we had been a there a week earlier she admitted, "I'm not really from Findlay, I'm from North Baltimore but nobody ever heard of it." I assured her I had heard of it, so she was a little skeptical about me the rest of the day.

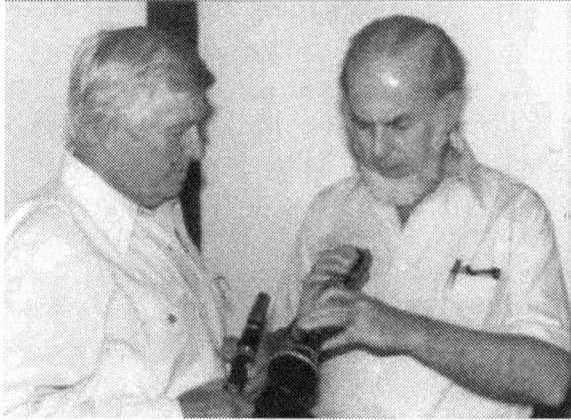

Gabe was in Tiffin, Ohio, with the Ezra Buzzington band out of Eaton in the 1920s and Marguerite was attending college there. Someone arranged for a couple of the girls to go out with two of the boys in the band and asked Marguerite which one she wanted to date. "The one with the white teeth," she replied, so a little over a week ago she and Gabe celebrated their 56th wedding anniversary.

Gabe's teeth are still white and so is his hair, but 80 years of adventurous living haven't dimmed the sparkle in his eye or added lines to his face. His step is as lively as ever, his fingers as nimble, his voice as steady and strong. When he was a boy, he said to the audience, someone told him to develop his voice by practicing singing in the toilet. "So I did," he said, "and before long they could hear me clear up at the house."

Gabe traveled far and wide as the Hoosier Hot Shots gained worldwide popularity, but he never lost his love for Indiana. The first song he played Saturday was "Back Home Again In Indiana." When the Hot Shots were entertaining troops overseas during World War II, he said, that was always the top request no matter what states those in the audience might be from.

123

Not long ago Gabe and Marguerite went out to dinner and found a picture of an old mill in Indiana on the cover of the menu. Gabe thinks it may be one he remembers as a boy in Knightstown. Later, while attending school in Indianapolis, James Whitcomb Riley visited his class. Gabe went on to another school in Alexandria and high school in Elwood.

Marguerite and Gabe were married in 1928 while the Buzzington band was playing the vaudeville circuit in New York. "Then," she says, "there was a six-week tour through New England, so it was our honeymoon."

And after that, of course, the years when the three young fellows from this part of the country formed their novelty band and soon rose to the top. Through it all, though – radio stardom, recording contracts, movies in Hollywood, television – Gabe and Marguerite remained what they had always been, an unaffected Hoosier boy and Buckeye girl. Gabe calls her, "My American Express – I won't leave home without her."

A unique twosome, Marguerite and Gabe Ward. A pair who never, as the years passed by, found time to grow old.

July 12, 1984

Mike Dague called after reading Monday's column in which three Hoosier Hot Shots were mentioned. He thought the group numbered four.

It did for a while, and for a short time there were five, including a female singer. Gabe Ward said it meant about a $500 drop in the weekly net profit.

At one time an official of Miles Laboratory in Elkhart, the group's sponsor, wanted them to add a trombone because he thought the sound was thin. "It was thin," Gabe said. "We weren't trying to sound like a 12-piece band. The trombone is a slide instrument and Hezzie already played a slide horn, so we wouldn't do it."

So during the years at the beginning and again later on, the Hoosier Hot Shots numbered only three – Gabe Ward, Hezzie and Ken Trietsch. All were members of Mark Schaefer's Ezra Buzzington's Rube Band when it broke up. They went to work as store help for Montgomery Ward in Lima and Van Wert,

Ohio and, at the same time, appeared without pay on WOWO in Fort Wayne. The station allowed them to plug personal appearances and the first was at the Elks Club in Van Wert. They earned $15 for a show and dance.

Gabe was interested in the route we followed to Battle Ground last Saturday. I told him we went through the towns where he attended school, Alexandria and Elwood and then Tipton.

"Is it still Route 28?" he asked.

I told him it was, so he said, "When I was in Alexandria they had a sign at the entrances to town – Not on the Nile but just as worthwhile."

I didn't tell him that kind of imagination is lacking in Alexandria today. Now you will find a sign reading "Small Town, U.S.A." What a comedown. At best it's insipid.

November 5, 1984

Gabe Ward, who wrote from his home in Encinitas, Calif. to say they can see snow on the distant mountains but the temperature of the Pacific is 66 degrees. The old Hoosier Hot shot again wishes he could smell the burning leaves in Indiana.

Gabe says he and wife Marge are getting ready for another rough winter. Sometime before it's over they might even have to put on sweaters or dig out a blanket.

He also took me to task for saying he's 80 because he won't be until Nov. 26. And he had a little to say about that well-known piece of classical music, "The Coat and Pants Do All the Work But the Vest Gets All the Gravy."

Here is something that is hard to understand. The Smithsonian wants Hezzie's old "Wabash Washboard" and so does the Country Music Hall of Fame in Nashville, but his wife prefers to have it in Indiana. Both she and Gabe have written to the Indiana Historical Museum in Indianapolis but neither has ever received a reply.

April 26, 1985

Someone from Gaston, but I don't know who, wrote to Gabe Ward looking for a record of the old Ezra Buzzington Band's recording of "Back to That Dear Old Farm." Gabe sent me a copy of the cover on the sheet music and the request reminded him of a couple of his favorites from the past – "The Coat and Pants Do All the Work But the Vest Gets All the Gravy" and "From the Indies to the Andes In His Undies." Genuine classics, and I remember them well.

Ol' Gabe wasn't feeling too good for a while but he's much better now. He's enjoying life at 80 in California, but at the same time still missing the good old days in Indiana.

MAY 24, 1985

Here is a question for the members of the Muncie Musicians Union: Whatever became of Bill Whitehurst?

Here is a question for educators: Should a talented kid be allowed to leave the classroom at 11 a.m. to pursue his talents, or would that violate too many rules?

Bill Whitehurst of Muncie was a clarinet man, and a good one from what I've heard. But he had an accident on a Friday morning in 1923 and the broken arm he suffered proved to be the big break for a high school youth in Elwood.

Bill was in a band and he had a tough assignment. It was up to him to play the melody because nobody else bothered with it. This was a band I've mentioned before, one formed in Eaton but billing itself as being from Muncie. Mark Schaefer was the leader of the zany bunch known as Ezra Buzzington's Rube Band. The sidemen who ignored all melodies were Guy Merrill and the several Trietsch brothers.

The band was booked for a weekend of performances at the Classic Theatre in Elwood. When Bill Whitehurst showed up with a broken arm the outfit was in big trouble. Schaefer made a few quick inquiries which resulted in the band members walking into Elwood High School at 11 o'clock in the morning. The situation was explained to those in authority, a

126

student who played clarinet was called from class and for two hours he rehearsed the numbers scheduled for the weekend.

That afternoon, much to his own surprise, rather than concentrating on his studies the student was carrying the tune for the band and performing solos at the Classic. It launched a long and illustrious musical career for the young Gabe Ward, one still going strong after more than 60 years.

But suppose the people in charge at Elwood High School had ordered the band from Muncie out of the building? What if they had said nothing was important enough to interfere with a young man's education?

No one can be sure of the answers, of course. Perhaps Gabe Ward would have found his way to the band eventually because he's the first to admit he was as zany as the rest of them. But he might not have. There's a good chance there would never have been a group known as the Hoosier Hot Shots. Who would have provided the spark for the WLS Barn Dance and filled the vacancy in Hollywood when the band appeared in all those movies?

We'll never know, but we can be certain that the course taken by popular music during the following decades would have been much different had some stiff-necked, unbending person been in charge at Elwood High School that morning.

So now that kid called out of class wonders whatever happened to Bill Whitehurst. He isn't even sure that Bill is still alive, but Gabe Ward says, "I'd love to know, and I'd love to thank him for it all. And of course I hope his arm is perfect! I never played as well as Bill."

Ol' Gabe had a question for me: Isn't there a lot of mystery in everyone's life?

February 5, 1986

At a time when gray days and unhappy events seem to dominate, that old Hoosier Hot Shot Gabe Ward passes along a few words of inspiration by an unknown author:

127

IN THE NEW YEAR MAY YOU HAVE –
Enough happiness to keep you sweet,
Enough trials to keep you strong,
Enough sorrows to keep you human,
Enough hope to keep you happy,
Enough failure to keep you humble,
Enough success to keep you eager,
Enough friends to give you comfort,
Enough wealth to meet your needs,
Enough enthusiasm to look forward,
Enough faith to banish depression,
Enough determination to make each
Day better than yesterday!

My needs are many and costly so I was doing pretty good until I hit the line about wealth. Ol' Gabe, the eternal optimist, sends greetings to all his Hoosier friends.

March 11, 1986

As promised, here is Gabe Ward's response to the subject of Monday's column, a rather scathing report on Muncie and Ball State by a San Diego newspaperman, Robert Scally:

Dear Friend,

"Life in the Last Lane" is more active at 6 a.m. today because of an article in my local paper, The Citizen.

It seems a certain Robert Scally wrote about Middletown U.S.A. with a feeling of worry about the future and students that may get a $25,000 per year entry-level job.

Being a born Hoosier with two Wabash relatives that are Ball State grads, I feel Scally contradicts the truth and dwells on "sour grapes" a lot. His finishing line is deplorable and is not funny or clever. He could use a sponsor to champion his cause.

David Letterman did not put Ball Sate on the map. My cousins and nephews and nieces did. They are so proud of having gone there.

Maybe I'm too jaded. I just think everybody should have a good feeling about Indiana and there is so much good to be

128

written about every state.   Lets have a big article somewhere about the many folks that became greats out of the one-room schoolhouses, the colleges and normal schools of Indiana.

I just can't explain my feelings since reading the article. I guess I'm too old to enjoy negative stuff. I love satire, but some things seem so unnecessary. Perhaps this letter is. Hopefully it will self-destruct in 10 seconds.

So Stodghill, have fun. Marguerite says she enjoyed Jackie's nice letter.

Scally is no Mike Royko. I will call on him soon. I get a kick out of things.

All the best,
Ol' Gabeeto

If anyone ever spread positive feelings it's Gabe Ward. All the Hoosier Hot Shots did that with their lively, fun-loving music that did so much to brighten the dark years of the Great Depression. And at 80, Gabe is still doing it.

Perhaps Robert Scally, that old scalawag, would find him unsophisticated, provincial, as he apparently found so many of us. But I don't think so. A few hours with Gabe might do more than anything else to show him that brains and formal education frequently fail to walk hand in hand. A few years under the guidance of a crusty Hoosier city editor such as the late Jack Richman would do him a world of good. Regardless, I think time and experience will teach him that a sharp knife is a useful instrument, but it needn't be used in either a coarse or cruel manner. With that, let us forgive him his trespasses against us.

* * *

But darn it, Ol' Gabe has put impossible ideas into my head. He and Marguerite are selling their condominium and I. would love to be its new occupant. He sent a real estate company handout and it sounds like a dream house in the closest thing I have found to paradise, San Diego.   The Wards plan to move to Oregon, but Gabe didn't say why. I honestly can't imagine.

If I could work deals with Gabe to take over his house and Robert Scally to take over his job, I would promise faithfully

129

to never write an unkind word about Muncie. That doesn't mean that in January I wouldn't gloat a little over the Midwest weather reports while enjoying a brew at an outdoor cafe. No one could deny a man that simple pleasure.

* * *

"The suicide song," do you remember it? Its real name is "Gloomy Sunday," something Jackie informed me of in one of those notes resulting from her research at the library.

OK, if you want to get technical about it, "Gloomy Sunday" was originally called "Szomoru Vasarnap." It still is in Hungary, where the song was written.

Paul Robeson introduced it in the U.S., but the best-selling record in 1941 was by Billie Holiday. It was advertised and promoted as "the suicide song" and a great many people took it to heart. Music, as most everyone knows, can lift you up or tear you apart. No need to say which effect "the suicide song" had on listeners.

You're probably dying to know (really, no pun intended), but I can't tell you how to pronounce Szomoru Vasarnap or even the name of its composer. I can, however, tell you what became of him. In 1968 he committed suicide.

September 19 1986

Gabe Ward, the old Hoosier Hot Shot, and his wife Marguerite have moved from sunny Southern California to Oregon. Their youngest son and Marguerite's sister live nearby. The address is 1349 Thompson Rd., Woodburn, OR 97071.

It didn't take the people of Woodburn long to discover Gabe. He already is being asked to perform, and Gabe seldom has to the asked twice. He's pleased, too, that a golf course is close by. The local newspaper, the Woodburn Independent, ran a lengthy feature on him in its Senior Life section.

"The area," writes Gabe, "is about as close to the Midwest feeling as you can get." Never having been there, I can't argue the point but seeing Mt. Hood in the background of a postcard he enclosed makes me wonder. Gabe, who always thinks of Indiana in the fall, says he hopes it is "as we like it."

130

Also enclosed was an ad from the 1939 New Year's Eve edition of the Evening Press. The Hot Shots were appearing on the stage at the old Wysor Grand Theater at Jackson and Mulberry. The movie on the same bill was "Henry Goes Arizona" with Frank Morgan, Guy Kibbee and Slim Summerville. There also was a travelogue on Peru, Fox News, and a Lew Lehr short. To see all this cost 40 cents, a dime for kids.

The Wysor Grand was opening its doors at 11:45 p.m. for a Gala New Year's Eve Show that included the Hoosier Hot Shots, Princess Adoree (Turkish Dream Dancer), Carl "Doc" Noble and his Goldcoasters Orchestra of Muncie, and the movie "The Day the Bookies Wept" starring Joe Penner and Betty Grable. All seats were 55 cents.

Joe Penner was a big radio comedian of the day, but died young. For a while it seemed everyone used his pet phrase, "Wanna buy a duck?"

On the back of the ad, Hudson and Pontiac were reporting record car sales, the best since 1928. Hudson had sold 10,250 cars in November, a rise of 77 percent over November 1938. Like Joe Penner, the Hudson died long ago.

A hit song at that time, I recall, was "Way Back in 1939 A.D." I wonder if they played it that night at the Wysor?

November 3, 1986

Gabe Ward, the old Hoosier Hot Shot, was back in Indiana for a few days in October. A letter written after he and his wife Marguerite – Marge for short – returned to Oregon was accompanied by a program from the Indiana Broadcasters Association awards ceremony. The top honor went to Gabe, who was named a Sagamore of the Wabash.

Considering how long the Hoosier Hot Shots served as goodwill ambassadors for Indiana it would be hard to name someone more deserving.

Gabe and Marge were kept busy throughout their visit, but had a great time. They came between the many October showers so Gabe said, "It's hard to describe how perfect Indiana was during our stay.

131

October 2, 1987

All things come to an end, even the good times and the laughter and the happy music. It is easy to forget that when you are having fun and the world around you is bright and exciting. But the days soon turn to years, the young grow old and eventually only the music remains.

You have to be an optimist to make music as the Hoosier Hot Shots made it. You have to be the sort of person that bounces back from adversity, that tries for the good but accepts the bad with a grin and sometimes must force a smile to hide a tear. Gabe Ward, last of the Hot Shots now, is trying to remember that and be as positive as possible about the death last month of Ken Trietsch, his friend and partner of more than 60 years.

Ken's last letter to Gabe was dated July 17. It bothered Gabe that the man who once began their tunes by turning to his brother Paul and saying, "Are you ready, Hezzie?" could no longer play golf or drive a car. When Ken died, as Hezzie had before him, it was time for Gabe to force one of those smiles and remember the good times they had. His eulogy for Ken Trietsch was simple and brief:

"My partner since vaudeville (1923-29), Montgomery Ward Stores (1929-32), WOWO Fort Wayne radio (1932-33), Chicago radio on NBC (1933-47), Hollywood movies (1939-50), World-wide bookings (1950-80).

"Now God has a better idea 'n' I'm glad He knows best.

"I was honored to be *Second Slide Whistle* and now I'll be pleased to join those in 'Washboard Heaven.'
END OF PARTNERSHIP."

But Gabe goes on making music and that of the Hoosier Hot Shots will still set toes to tapping long after all of us are gone. Only a special few leave such a legacy.

March 24, 1988

From even further west comes another of the always welcome letters from Gabe Ward, last of the Hoosier Hot Shots now that Ken and Paul Trietsch are dead. Paul's nickname gained fame throughout the world in that familiar line: "Are you ready, Hezzie?"

Gabe reminisced a bit about their early days on Keith's, Loew's, Orpheum, and Pantages vaudeville circuits from 1923 through 1929 when the boys who became the Hoosier Hot Shots played with Ezra Buzzington's Rube Band out of Eaton. He wrote, "I have four sides we recorded at Starr Piano Co., Gennett label, Richmond, Ind., in 1925!"

The later success of the Hot Shots is well documented, but Gabe brings out an unusual side of the story. "Nothing much has been written to praise high school dropouts but I can truthfully say plenty of opportunity exists for those with enough ambition and hard work to find decent companions and always save a few dimes!"

Through good times and bad on radio, television and more than 20 movies, too, when he was making whatever he could with his $35 clarinet and doing whatever else came along, including selling newspapers.

And he saved memories as well. He put it this way:

"What price glory? I am completely bogged down among my souvenirs! My fourth garage sale in as many years will be soon. Most of the stuff does not interest the offspring. When we go to visit the marrieds it's like we never left since they already have so much of our old furniture, etc. etc. – lots of etcetera! What they don't have are so many wonderful memories I have secured through public service, press folks and audiences from far and wide. So much attention is awesome as I sit here and have total recall."

November 25, 1988

A card from the far off Willamette Valley in Oregon reminded me that Gabe Ward, the only surviving member of the Hoosier Hot Shots, still misses the smell of burning leaves in Indiana every autumn. Gabe, who played clarinet and sang with the Trietsch brothers of Delaware County in the popular group, celebrated his 84th birthday yesterday.

He still plays the clarinet, of course, and still gets a lot of mail from Indiana. And he says there are many Hoosiers living nearby in the Williamette Valley. He thinks it's a great place but his roots remain in Indiana.

July 7, 1989

Jackie says I goofed. Not that this is unusual, understand. But this time she was speaking of a specific goof.

That's a dangerous line for me to leave hanging in the air. The other day while struggling to put together one of those easy-to-assemble gadgets I said, "Hold this nut." She grabbed my arm.

Now, however, she is justly upset. I forgot to mention that June 30 was the 61st wedding anniversary of Marguerite and Gabe Ward, the lone surviving Hoosier Hot Shot. Had I done so when she told me to, people could have sent them anniversary cards. After all, they've been married nearly as long as I've been alive and that's a long, long time. But the real reason they deserve recognition is that Gabe and Marge are two of the nicest people around, true ambassadors of goodwill for Indiana wherever they go. Ohio, too, because Marguerite is a native Buckeye. So was Hoosier humorist Herb Shriner, who said he wasn't born in Indiana but came here as soon as he heard about it. He didn't stick around long, though, if the truth is to be known.

Anyway, in case anyone wants to send a belated greeting, the Wards' address is ... oops, scratch my first entry. I can't imagine how these goofs occur. Jackie's explanation shall be disregarded in the interest of harmony.

So here it is, the correct, up-to-the-minute address of Marguerite and Gabe Ward: 1580 Newburg Highway, Apartment 19, Woodburn, Ore. 97071. No goof-ups here, take it from me.

October 18, 1989

At his age Milton Berle claims to have done just about everything in his beeveedees and at my age I've received just about everything in the mail. Or so I thought, but then a buckeye arrived from Oregon and that was a refreshing change.

I was well on my way toward finishing up boyhood before discovering that beeveedees was not the correct name for shorts worn by men. You heard the word all the time. In thinking back on it I wonder why there was so much talk about underwear. Some men wore jockey shorts, but there again it took a while for me to realize it is Jockey with a capital J because, like B.V.D., it is a brand name.

So popular was the expression beeveedees that the word made it into both the Dictionary of Slang and Euphemism and the Pocket Dictionary of American Slang. Today, unless I'm missing out on it, there is far less talk about what men are wearing under their pants. Or trousers, which is another word seldom heard today outside clothing stores.

As for buckeyes, they inspire thoughts of Ohio, not Oregon. They have them there, it appears, because that old Hoosier Hot Shot Gabe Ward sent one to me. This, I think, was because his wife Marguerite is from Ohio.

Gabe loves the smell of burning leaves in autumn. Without fail it inspires thoughts of boyhood days in Alexandria and Knightstown, which he refers to as K-town.

"My favorite season is here," he wrote, "and it does bring to mind the smell of leaves burning, that famous 'When the Frost Is On th' Punkin' and days long ago that had us singing 'Roses of Picardy,' 'Keep the Home Fires Burning,' 'K-K-Katy' and always some Irving Berlin sheet music to place on the old 'pie-anna' during winter house parties! And it was quite an experience to 'Model-T' ourselves to Muncie from Alexandria. Going by interurban was really first-class. You could meet new people and chat."

And I'm sure he did. As Jackie put it, "Gabe is one of those men who truly loves people."

Enclosed was a copy of the sheet music for the song "Down Among the Sugar Cane" along with this explanation:

"Dick, my first recording with Buzzingaton's Band was at the Starr Piano Co. in Richmond, Ind. in April 1925 on the Gennett Label. Mark Schaefer (Ezra Buzzington) of Eaton sang it but no one had the music. Recently I found a copy in a pawn shop. Fortunately I obtained a record of it from the recording master at Richmond."

135

Not having the music never kept a musician of Gabe's breed from belting out a song. Some great ones couldn't even read music so having it would have been of no use at all. Bunny Berigan comes to mind. If a finer trumpet player ever lived I haven't heard him. He lead his own orchestra, was first trumpeter with Tommy Dorsey and other leading big bands and got along just fine without reading music.

When he was nine, Bunny Berigan's grandfather gave him his first trumpet. "Here," he said, this is you. Play you." Bunny took him at his word.

Gabe Ward and the Hoosier Hot Shots recorded five songs that made it to the charts of top hits. The first was "Breezin' Along With the Breeze" in 1937. That was followed during the next two years by "Red Hot Fannie," "The Man With the Whiskers" and "Annabelle" Then in 1946 came a hit on the Decca label, "Someday (You'll Want Me T Want You)," with Sally Foster handling the vocal. **(Note: it was Gil Taylor)**

Those, of course, were not necessarily the top favorites of Hot Shot fans any more than Gabe's trip to Europe and North Africa to entertain troops was his favorite. Instead, he wrote, it was "going via interurban from Alexandria thru Linwood to Anderson to Indy – then thru Irvington and Greenfield to K-town. An absolutely great trip – better than my time in Casablanca, Oran, Algiers, Italy, Austria. Ha! Ha!"

Gabe is spending his 80s selling audio and video cassettes of the Hot Shots and being a good husband. "After 61 years," he says, "I know how. Forgive my self-grandizement. Is that a word? I was *wont* to use it! Ha! Ha!

"Squirrels n' Nuts n' Leaves – we love it! We hope n' cope."

You encounter many optimists along life's pathways but I have never met one who could top Gabe. He recalls the old days with pure pleasure, never allowing his memories to get in the way of today's fun and enjoyment. But it was a serious Otto "Gabe" Ward who posed for a postcard photo in 1909 while wearing one of the big Fauntleroy bowties forced upon young boys. Under the picture he wrote: "Hello Uncle Claude. When are you coming home to see me. I am just as bad as I look. Your nephew." Bad? Mischievous, maybe.

*   *   *

The majority of the preceding "columns" are obviously excerpts although a few were complete in themselves. Other letters from Gabe just as he wrote them are found in the following chapter. Among them is one written two days before his death. Much of the material in the columns is repetitious as it also can be found in the text of this book.

Few column subjects sparked as much interest as those featuring the Hoosier Hot Shots. As the three original members of the group were from the Muncie area that could be expected. Strangely enough, the residents of the city displayed little interest in the career of another local man, Orville Harrold, although he gained worldwide fame as a lead tenor in the Metropolitan Opera. It seems that the more down home music of the Hot Shots had far more appeal than did opera.

Gabe was dead wrong in thinking I knew something about clarinets. My own musical accomplishments were limited to fooling around with an ocarina and a kazoo.

Of the many things he wrote with never a complaint, the only one that came close was the sentence, "A type of lonesomeness exists" in a September 13, 1990 letter. For a man who loved people and cherished the years with his wife, loneliness would have been difficult for him to endure. Those five words speak volumes about one peril of growing old.

GABE'S OWN ACCOUNT OF HIS LIFE AS HE TOLD IT TO ME. IT RAN IN THE MUNCIE EVENING PRESS
(Most of this is repetitious as it appeared earlier in the text)

"When things got tough in vaudeville and theaters were putting in all movies and no stage shows, Paul (Hezekiah) Trietsch, Ken (Rudy Vaselino) Trietsch and Otto (Gabe Hawkins) Ward quit 'Ezra Buzzington's Comedy Rube Band.' That Ezra had nothing to do with Ezra P. Watters (real name Pat Barrett) who was on local WLS Chicago Prairie Farmer station doing a 15-minute stint for Pinex Cough Syrup. Ezra Buzzington's real name was Mark Schaefer.

"I have been the official publicist and P.R. man all these years and have a worldwide 'pen pal' relationship with fans.

Many erroneous quotes have been in print but, thank God, the intent invariably has been good. We have made millions happy with zany, fun-tastic renditions, kidded the operas with our Corn-certs and my present mail is stacked up because of the good ol' nostalgia from our 15 years on the NBC Network Alka-Seltzer shows. Who else, of course, would we work for but Dr. Miles Laboratories in Elkhart, Ind. We were their boys!

"We started out with a handshake and soon had a contract worth $1,000 each Saturday night live from the Eighth Street Theater in Chicago. Admission was 85 cents to see these broadcasts. There were 1,200 seats and they were sold out weeks in advance.

"I could do a whole story about the 'National Barn Dance' movie by Paramount. Another whole story about our 22 pictures at Columbia and our first movie at Republic with Gene Autry (not a western).

"A beautiful movie was written just for us about Indiana during the war in 1942. It was "Hoosier Holiday" with Dale Evans. A victory garden thing ending with a grand parade and the Hoosier Hot Shots in an electric auto!

"Now about the Rosedale story. Radio Station E.Z.R.A., the powerful little five-watter down in Coles County, Ill. was entirely mythical and was really a soap opera. Folks took it to their hearts, sent in money to the depicted characters, and so much mail came that the post office set up a sub-station near Mattoon, Ill. The song 'Rosedale, Everyone's Hometown' was our sign-off each time. I did sub-tone clarinet behind Uncle Ezra's recitation, Hot Shot music and dialogue constituted a major part of the program.

"Mark Schaefer of Eaton, Ind. started and financed his 'Ezra Buzzington's Rube Band' with the aid of several Trietsch brothers and came to the old Classic Theater in Elwood to appear for three days. Bill Whitehurst of Muncie, on clarinet, broke his arm and I was picked to replace him. In October 1923 I left Elwood and the band went to the Terrace Theater in Danville, Ill. From then on we played countless fairs and theaters – Pantages, Keith-Orpheum circuits, Hippodrome in New York and years of headline contracts until 'bustin' up in 1929.

"Crash! Nothing! Hezzie, Ken and Gabe, the Three Hot Shots, went to work as Montgomery Ward store help in Lima and Van Wert, Ohio. We stuck together and went on WOWO (Fort Wayne) radio for no pay but were allowed to plug any personal engagements we could get. Our first day was at the Elks Club in Van Wert -- $15 for a show and dance. I could do a feature story about all the charity events we did for Red Cross, etc.

"Dick, you must be worn out by now. I hate to quit. You see I'm the active one and appear at colleges doing my Hoosier Orator bit and workshops on Early American jazz. I have

139

compiled a discography of all the 150 recordings and radio shows we did and am busy sending albums and cassettes around the world.

"My first love has always been the printed page and secondly, radio. I delivered Dr. Miles Almanac door to door when I was in grade school at Alexandria. I was born in Knightstown, Henry County, and not Warsaw. Ha! Ha!!

"Loved your column and appreciate it immensely. Thanks for it all. Hope to meet you sometime and do a 'gig' in Muncie. Regards to the Press staff – I love good journalism. Don't forget to write. – Gabe"

The story was published in 1983. Gabe went on to say that he and Ken still saw each other. Also mentioned in the story were letters from two nieces of Ken and Hezzie, Adrienne Current and Lavenna Putnam. The latter had recently visited Ken in California and took the earlier *In the Press of Things* columns about the Hoosier Hot Shots so he could see them.

There was a letter, too, from Mrs. Edmond Spray, daughter of Mark Schaefer. She told about his days as Ezra Buzzington and his association with Hezzie, Ken and Gabe.

So in Indiana the Hoosier Hot Shots were both remembered and loved.

LETTERS FROM GABE

If ever there was a man who enjoyed writing letters it was Gabe Ward. A sampling of the many he wrote to me are included here.

For the "Ward File" or "Self-Destruction" (Shredding)

Hoosier Hot Shot
Columbia Pictures
and Records

C. O. "Gabe" Ward
307 Harrisburg Drive
Encinitas, CA 92024
(619) 942-1075

June 15th 1987 — *(mostly an ad-lib early A.M. Clarinet Happy Ending)*

Dear Friends,

"I was looking at that picture of Dick looking over my German made albert system Clarinet" Dick's good wife snapped the two of us in an apparent serious mood — I regret that we did not pursue that conversation a bit further but everything seemed so hurried at Tippecanoe Battle-Field gathering that day in 1984. (3 yrs ago)

Over the years I've been asked why I didn't get an up to date improved system. Some indicated I might have been fairly great on the Clarinet if I had studied! I sure have appreciated it all but I have learned some hard facts. Marguerite n' I were to have been married in Toledo ohio on this day June 15. 1928 — I was in Ezra Buzzingtone Rube Band of Eaton-Indiana n' appearing at the old opera House in St. Louis, four shows a day, 85.00 per week. We were head-lined — played poker between shows, never took off our make-up all the time to go eat etc. I was having a new H. + M. wardrobe trunk made at the St. Louis factory,

141

#. It had an ironing board, jewel box, shoe box, and special His n' Her drawers! Really tops for our trip to New York and Eastern Vaudeville on Loew's Circuit! I had an old Clarinet! I lost so much in 5 + 10¢ poker that I set the wedding up to June 30th at Toledo. Stayed at the Secor Hotel on our wedding time and then to Napoleon Ohio on the Maumee River for a four day date. We packed 'em in + were held over 2 days. Made over 100°° each (8 people) on percentage. The old Clarinet duets with Heggie's whistle were big stuff on "Yearning" "Margie". I wanted to buy a new Clarinet! at the Pedler factory and others in Elkhart, the average price was in the 90°° range! But, I was married now! Went to New York with the old horn n' new Marge. Folks said they liked a strong melody and I made a good sound. I guess I believed them and kept the old Clarinet! I did buy a spare from a pawn shop for 35°°. Later I sold it to my Indianapolis cousin for 35°°. That was about 1938 I think. I don't suppose he will ever pay me! Ha! Ha! "He's a good ol' Hoosier" after all these years, here's the pay-off—June 11th. I started some repair work on my very 1st Clarinet - a 13-key-2 ring High Pitch from France. My Uncle Dewey Ward played it in the Indianapolis News Boys Band

IH. in 1909-10-11.

He brought it to me in Alexandria in 1917. It hung in our Coal Shed for a year before I found I could get some instruction at the Hi-School. 35¢ per lesson and I became really interested. In six months I was on 3rd clarinet on easy stuff. Then I began to love the old clarinet.

June 13th I recieved a call from Dale Ogden Historian at Indiana State Museum + Hall of Fame – He's from Warsaw and is involved in things about Historic sites etc. a nice man to know, 202 No. Alabama St – 317-232-1637 – Back to my old system Clarinet – Its on its way to adorn a spot on the Museum's Walls next to "Are You Ready Hezzie" Washboard & other Hoosier Hot Shot Memorabilia. I'm expecting prints of Oct. 1986 Conference, So Dick, tonite I'm to entertain the Presbyterian Men's Club. "With the old system Clar. n' my "New System Wife" of June 30 - 1928 – will stay home – Ha Ha 'Our best wishes and appreciation to you both" Ol' System Gabe –

P.S. – D. My New-Lite pick-up truck at FT. Wayne is called "The Hoosier Hot Shot" "Hope its as good as the old Clar." Ha Ha

Much of the material in this letter and those that follow is repetitious as it also is found in the text. Seeing the words just as Gabe put them on paper provides a better picture of this optimistic, outgoing man than reading bits and pieces in cold type can ever do.

HOT-SHOT-FILE

C. O. "Gabe" Ward
503-982-1821
Hoosier Hot Shot
Columbia Pictures
and Records

C.O. GABE WARD
2233 COUNTRY CLUB TERRACE
WOODBURN, OR 97071

Saturday 2-20-'88

Dear Friends,

"What Price Glory"? I am completely bogged down among my Souvenirs! My 4th garage sale, in as many years, will be soon. Most of the stuff does not interest the offspring. When we go to visit the marrieds, it's like we never left since they already have so much of our old furniture etc: etc: - Lots of Etcetera! What they don't have are so many wonderful memories I have secured through public service, press folks and audiences from far n' wide! So much attention is awesome as I sit here n' have "total recall". Even General Motors Chevy trucks and Northeast Indiana dealers have a new one called "The Hoosier Hot Shot". Sounds like a basket-ball team. Ha! Ha! So far I can't get any response from Ft. Wayne G. M. Marketing. With all the promotion scheduled for Hoosiers in 1988, I hope to come back for something. I have some contacts now. Anyway, I'll be looking toward 60 yrs. in "The Wonderful World of Marguerite" come June 30!

Nothing much has been written to praise

144

II (DROP-OUTS)

C.O. "Gabe" Ward

Hoosier Hot Shot
Columbia Pictures
and Records

Hi-school "drop-outs" but I can truthfully
say, "plenty of opportunity exists" for those
with enough ambition and hard work to
find decent companions and always save a
5% few dimes! In Muncie, Anderson, Alexandria,
Elwood, Kokomo, Ft. Wayne, Warsaw and all
over Indiana, I made a few bucks with the
old 35°° Clarinet and selling newspapers. The
weekly Saturday Blade & Chicago Ledger and
Lone Scout magazine were good for about
four dollars a week 1917-18-19- WOW!
Lippincott lamp chimney factory 6°° for eleven
four hour turns a week @ 55¢ per turn.
So Dick, how can your mysteries contain as
much intrigue as I've had in being a Hoosier?
But, I've never read one! - forgive me!
Marguerite never told me to quit the music
biz. She was not a drop-out, attended Tiffin
Ohio business College, was a secretary in
Toledo when we married. Her 20°° per week
salary sure helped out when Buzzington's
Rube Band of Eaton, In. was not booked.
Mark Shaeffer (Epa) had a farm at Farmland

145

C. O. "Gabe" Ward

Hoosier Hot Shot
Columbia Pictures
and Records

and could retreat to it and enjoy "laying off". We usually borrowed some from him to get to the next engagement! He was a gentleman and a pal to us all! His daughter Eloise Spray lives in Muncie somewhere. 1200⁰⁰ per week on Keith's, Loews, Orpheum, Pantages Vaudeville circuits in 1923-5- to 1928. Was meat. We had a super novelty type, *confused jazz* bunch o' Hicks! I have four sides we recorded at Star Piano Co Gennet Label Richmond, Ind. 1925!

So, I'm a genuine "*Wandering Hoosier*" and doing about thirty pieces of mail per week to Indiana, Ohio + Illinois folks. Thanks to Muncie Press for being so nice. My first love has always been the newspaper. I delivered DR. Miles Almanac - door to door for years! "More *Ups* than *Downs*" Marge sends her kindest thoughts and this ol' "drop-out" wishes you the same!

"Gabe - at *random*" (that's near gaston)
Ha! Ha!

Gabe's mention of being a Wandering Hoosier referred to a weekly column I wrote at the same time I was cranking one out every day for the Muncie Evening Press. The Wandering Hoosier ran in twenty-five Indiana and regionals newspapers including the Chicago Tribune.

146

7 A.M. - 5-11-1988.

Hi Dick 'n Jackie" - I miss knowing about you and I've known that "nobody owes me a letter". Also I am certain that a good way to have a friend is, "to be one". So, I am wont to sit right down 'n write to you. Still don't own a typewriter but found a flock of good pens at a Sears Surplus Store, 12 for a buck! Ha! Ha! Imagine

OVAH

all the fun I can have with those! It's been a few years since I met you at the Battle Ground affair and when I look at that photo of you holding my Clarinet, I wonder what went through your mind. I had a hunch that you knew a little bit about Clarinets. My 1st one is now occupying space at Indy Hall of Fame alongside Hezzie's Washboard. I'm sending the Hot Shot Drum set. I'm a member of Indiana State Museum Society 202 N. Alabama St. Folks can see the Hoosier Hot Shot Case there and visit the Museum Shop.

Ah! the Ravages of Time - So much happens! Since the Oregonian Story I'm swamped with phone calls, letters and visitors. Seems Indiana moved out here! I've helped open a radio station, have done 8 hrs. filming for P.B.S for a

147

Prime-Timers T.V. shows and mailed some 800=
of cassettes n' Nostalgic stuff! Sooo, "Busy Busy"
is the name of the game.
   My Hoosier mail is almost like a chain letter.
Folks ask me to write to some friend or
relative and I do. I write for handicaps that
can't - They tell me "one on one" things - extremely
interesting! Dr. Strother, retired head of
Drama Dept. Ball State has Hoosier Hot Shot
memorabilia in Ball State library archives.
   So, I'm about out of "Anecdotes" for now.
Its early morning, I love it! Marge still
asleep! My part of a church event will
find me doing "When the Saints" "Closer Walk"
and "Amazing Grace" - All on Bass Clarinet.
I'm doing a clarinet cassette - Many requests
thru the years! "Knock it off Gabe"
"Dick - you may add this to your shredder" -
"Be a politician" Ha! Ha! Gabe n'
                                    Marge
                           60 YRS - JUNE 30-'8.

The beginning of this letter was Gabe's gentle way of
reminding me that I hadn't written to him for quite some time.
Unlike Gabe, I hated writing letters and excused this failure by
saying I had to write all day on the job and had run out of
words by quitting time.

148

"Gabe's Anecdotes" + "Randoms"

Life after 20 - Life after 40 - Life after 60 - Life after 80 - Where will it change? To sum it up in a nut-shell, it's just been one grand trip into the wonderful, magical world of "Marguerite". The past 20 months has allowed me to do a whole bunch of serious thinking along with that same old line that permeates my body 'n soul from as far back as I remember. I love today but I love to recall the times that I carried wood 'n coal to build a fire for Daddy Phillips at the big school on the hill at Innisdale. He was a kind 'n gentle, pot bellied man who could blow a mean pitch pipe to start our school day with "Flow Gently Sweet Afton" or "Columbia The Gem of the Ocean", A flag salute, a prayer and then some education. four grades in the big school room, 4 in the little school about 3 blocks away. Stella Pentecost Ward from the town + covered bridge area of Matthews was a well known Mother + sometimes mid-wife, wet nurse + beloved by all of mankind. Kids got satisfaction from that lady when they needed it! She was our Mother - un-educated basically but surely "a Saint".

I like to sit 'n think about life in a 3 room house with a summer kitchen, 3 lots of garden, toilet out back or in a secluded corner of a room, a dug well, frozen pump handles, some manure around the house foundation to help

"You may shred, just like politicians do." The "junior family" Grandale - a suburb of Alexandria is a great story of Early 1900 Va. picture

"I'm a "for sure" Wandering Hoosier"

insulate, long stockings over our shoes, to trudge
about a mile thru the snow to school. a
foot log across Pipe Creek on the way to down
town Alexandria. I met old man Sawyer who
invented Rock Wool from Indiana lime stone in
his Quarry. Dad Ward wheeled that stone up
ramps @ 1 25 per ten hour day! He let me
have fire-wood from his Mineral Wool
factory. I lied about my age, at 13 I was
big n' strong enough to work at Lippincott's
Glass & chimney Factory at Alexandria, I was
supposed to be 14 yrs. old. 55¢ for each
4 hours work or $6 05 for a weeks work. Too
much! Mother got it all but 1 00 - She
washed n ironed for the Jimmy Wales family.
1 25 for both - he was Mayor of Alexandria
and a distant 2nd or 3rd cousin. We could
get by O.K. - went to 1st Christian Church.
I could do volumes about anderson, Muncie
Daleville, Marion, Fairmount, Summitville
Warsaw + the lakes, Elwood, Tipton, Noblesville, Cicero, My Hoosier Melody Five was
an attraction from "Roses of Picardy" + Keep The
Home Fires Burning, K-K-K-Katy - of course
"Alexander's Rag time" Band and "Over There"
never left the Charts. To do a gig

More Notes n' Anecdotes
from 1st Clarinet n' Second slide whistle
of the original H.H.S.

All Summer at Kosiosko County Lakes @ 25⁰⁰
per week plus room n' board was
absolutely tops. To own a Saxophone
in 1920-1-2-3-4 was really Big n' wild.
People were wanting Saxophones - Boy
was I glad I had a C Melody and
Could play from sheet music and
didn't need to transpose! Haffa!
So, in answer to my query about, what to
expect after 80, Id like to comment
that "what we do is what we are and
its mostly our fault if we don't "just
do it".
Marguerite n' I do "What we can - With
what we have - Where we are - Aint
Bad"
1988 gave me splendid news mentions and
in 1989 I'll break my neck to thank
the publications for remembering me and
the Hoosier Hot Shots!
All we wanted to do was cheer
up the AM crash victims! It worked!
So just to mention some of my
favorite folks "Thank you Jackie n
Dick Stodghill of Muncie Evening Press
for being so nice! As ever
Th. Write Stuff   Hoosier Hot Shot "Gabe'

151

New address - 1580 NEWBURG·HI·WAY
"Th' Write Stuff"   APT·19   4-26-1989

"6 am - my Quiet Time."
60º Beautiful Springtime"   C.O. "Gabe" Ward
                                     503-982-1821
"In the Hay-Loft of my mind"   Hoosier Hot Shot
Ha! Ha!   Columbia Pictures
                                     and Records

Dear Friend Dick,
hopefully, you n' Jackie n' cohorts at the paper are
in good spirits n' enjoying the 1st hundred days
of our new bunch in Washington D.C. It seems
so many are accused of being "tainted" like some
old frozen stuff in your fridge. Don't know if
we should eat it or throw it out! Anyway Gee
always contend, that the Indiana, Hoosier and Midwest experience that I know has made me love my
country more than influences in our Capitol! I'm
great for local government and dollar a year
Volunteers! Don't Know if I'm smart or plain
dumb! If I spent too much time, I'd feel like a
criminal, or Killing Time would make me a type
of murderer! So, this day while Marge sleeps, I'm
longing to talk to friends, by pen! I'm far more
interested in your back yard fence n' squirrels
than nuts in D.C. God Bless Them! Hoosiers are
blessed by the very name - it denotes a fine
traditional fondness for things n' folks! I
have a box filled with written thoughts from
as far back as 1923 when I joined Mark
Shaffer's Buzzington's Rube Band. Recently, I discovered a great Sheet Music Copy of that very
1st recording session at Richmond-Gennett
                         studios 1925. Buzzington had

152

"TRIVIA TWO" Jackie: Marge 82 yrs. on april 29

C. O. "Gabe" Ward

Hoosier Hot Shot
Columbia Pictures
and Records

a great baritone voice
and sang "Illustrated Songs" for silent movies.
We learned "Down Among The Sugar Cane" from
him n' his Banjo. Never saw the music - now I
have a copy. If interested I'll Zerox you a
copy! And send you a recording!

Stodghill, I'm busy, busy these days, more music
gigs than I should do, sold my house so -
no lawn, taxes, leaky roofs etc - full time as
help for Marguerite n' music stuff. about
75 letters so far in april - quite a few want
my Videos which contain a Gabe Ward + H.H.S
Profile as seen on A.B.C + Cable. plus a 1944
Soundies Film of The K.P. Serenade - Comedy
army + washboard epic! Ha Ha!

about time to do the Insulin + medicine for
Marge - Come June 30 - "61 yrs married" Ha!
When I look at you fingering my Clarinet at
Battle ground - it appears that you knew about
it! Did you play an instrument?
          "Our Best to you both"

P.S. I'm doing special "Class - B - Union tapes - One man got
14 - each is very personal from him to them via me!
Time consuming but "Original + Surprising!

153

The following four pages of notes were written on a folded restaurant placemat. Gabe didn't believe in wasting paper.

Work Sheet 'Please Shred'

S. Todgehill
900 W. Cromer Ave
Muncie — In. 47303

The Ever
— Falling Leaves — Since 1984 when
we meat at B.G
Burning the Leaves from the
boxes and the attic of my mind

and since before that when those
nice articles "In The Press" and
in "The Wandering Hoosier" helped
kick out so many Hoosier Hot SHoT
followers. Surely they are the best
folks in the world. Now I'm into
the "Burning of the leaves from the
boxes + the attic of My Mind" How can
I bear to discard an old vaudeville
program from Keith Theatre or a pictur
of th' Lyric at Indianapolis — shots
of the Indiana Theatres at Marion —
Evansville — Terre Haute etc.
The Keith Theatre at Toledo — 1927
where we had

154

4/8 x 10's of Buzzington's Rube Band with all their odd assortment of instruments. Many were made by the 5 Trietsch Bros who lived on a farm out of Muncie. Joe was a pattern maker at G.M. in Pontiac Mich + fashioned wood into Saxaphone Trumpet + Slide Trombone etc - Ezra Buzzington was Mark Shafer of Eaton where we rehearsed to go to the New York + down east vaudeville houses. Ken Trietsch played an Eb recording BASS - Because it was big + a hassle to travel with Ken got 15⁰⁰ per week more than the others, Ezra + wife Ola got 1500⁰⁰ per week for the act - Paul ~~~~~~~~~~~ on alto Horn + slide whistle got 90⁰⁰ per week. Fred Ferg on trombone of Muncie, got 75⁰⁰ - I did all the leads on Clar. "SAX- I got 85⁰⁰ - It was the hot shot Novelty, comedy, band in all of vaudeville + got smash reviews! Eventually Ezra

3/ retired on his farm at
Farmland Ind.

a few years later he was my
house guest during the house
warming of my new home in
Chicago a showplace at 16,000
I might add. (1941) Sold for a bunch
when we moved to Hollywood
in 1946!

Dick, where were you in 1945?
Just got the Enclosed News reprint
from Sam De Vincent of W.O.W.O.
I have supplied him with copy &
tunes thru the years my mail
from his listeners on the "Little
Red Barn Sunday show, has kept me
busy sending letters, cassettes and
now, fortunately, I have 2 full length
H.H. Shot Columbia Pictures 1946. With
us as the stars + Ken Curtis (who
became Festus on gunsmoke) these
films started us on a lucrative

156

6 yrs. contract —

All those clippings from Billboard
Variety, Clipping services, even a
lot of Gabe Ward stories! My 1st
love was the News Media via
newspapers. I delivered DR Miles
Almanac at Alexandria in 1915-
16-17 — I liked to walk into the
Press room + get — I came out
with some nice space for the H.H.S.
by doing that. I still hear from
a few old operators!

Dick, "I'm being carried away"
So, all I really want is to thank
you "n" Jackie for being good
friends. If you have a video.
I'll send you a V.C.R.

1990 has been hectic — both of
us hospitalized for 4 months.
Now we're adjusting + enjoying
mail + visits from old W.h.S
+ alka seltzer 'n' Movie fans —
"Our best to you always"
Gabe.

157

7 A.M. - "My Quiet Time" "Marge Sleeps" "Pen-sive Mood"

C.O. "Gabe" Ward
1-503-982-1821
Hoosier Hot Shot
Columbia Pictures
and Records

Dear Friends Dick n' Jackie,

"thanks for your nice remembrance". Seems just a short while since we met at Battle Ground and I long to visit Indiana again! Too many "Ifs" "Ands" n' Buts" kept me away. However the good ol' Hoosier Hospitality stays alive in so many ways via phones, letters n' Cassettes. Your greeting occupies a prominent spot in our new apartment. Muncie, Marion, Columbus, Fairmount Ft. Wayne - Roanoke - Shelbyville, La Grange mail is to be taken care of this week along with Ohio, New Jersey and Jenks Oklahoma! Some photos of Cole Porter's Seven Pillars estate at Peru came. Ney Ohio dairy farmers write me volumes about their families, aches n' pains! I love it! My mail is better than reading a book!

A Portland Oregonian paper survey maintains that Portland is the most courteous city in the U.S. Another article says folks are sick of hearing "Have a Nice Day". Ha Ha!. Of course nobody asked me! Sam DeVincent + Nancy and the "Hill-Topers" of WOWO always talk about the "Golden Goodies" and ol' Gabe n' Marge - We met

In Chicago years ago and did some bookings together, I have given him copy and recordings for years and now he sends listeners my address. I am always selling tapes n' my new Videos To Hoosiers. "Fiddlin' Jim Raines" of Elwood just phoned + talked about 50 minutes. Hunter Goins from Columbus, In. knocked on our door, he is a teacher and a Marathon runner. Used to teach at Dunreith and knew much about Knightstown where I was born. I can go on n' on about the hundreds of Hoosiers that are the most courteous n' lovable folks on my planet! Enclosed you have a copy of another "gig" I am doing! A personal tape from your old Class Mates is great for those that have everything. You know about Pugsley — he sent a big list of 1938 Class - names, places n' Data - I made a script + did each tape differently + put on "Back Home again In Ind" + "Amazing Grace" on the Bass Clarinet. Some orders bring as much as 200°. "HallMark Watch Out Ha Ha.

Well folks, "Enuff is Enuff" Thanks again + on to our 62nd Gabe

"Hoosier Hot Shot - Cods off" 2-21-1990

Dear Friend Dick,

how are things in good ol' Delaware County? Through my Hoosier grape vine I keep quite well informed and my circle of friends keeps getting larger. I love that and I don't get bored like a lot of Seniors do! Some say "Death i' Taxes are the sure things. I'd like to add to that by saying " The only constant thing is Change! It happens to all of us all the time and for sure!

Jan. 28th I was doing "Beautiful Dreamer" on my Bass Clarinet at a big Celebration of a ladies 100th birthday. She loves the Stephen Foster things. I ran out of wind excused myself and had a big change, I had a heart attack. Marge i' I are in separate assisted living quarters for possibly 6 to 8 weeks until we can evaluate our situations. I'm great, do tread mill etc and only one Nitro Pad per day No pills and wouldn't you know, my fans i' friends provide me with the greatest therapy of all! So much Love i'

160

attention! I can't help but to get well! Sam DeVincent my long time WoWo - 7T Wayne producer of "Sunday Little Red Barn Show" for over 40 yrs. called me and has given my address to dozens who buy my tapes n' now my feature length videos of Columbia films of 1946. Baby Boomers provide a whole new market! So, I'll still dig out Memorabilia for lots of Collectors, Hoosier Friends and even West Germany folks!

This ol' "Sagamore of the Wabash" hopes to scribble n' scratch for many years! I am 'wont' to treasure our meeting at Battle-ground in 1987. Marge n' Jackie looked so nice!

Dick, before I'm carried away by too much talk, let me say thanks for "Muncie Quotes" "Wandering Hoosier" Etc. "Hope the beautiful Indiana Spring will soon be upon you". "Hello Jackie"

Cordially,
Ol' Gabe
1990

P.S. "I can't toot or drive my car for a while" Ha Ha!

Phone - 503-691-2924

Marge n' I did our 61st anni -
North Baltimore Ohio
+
ELWOOD - IND
"quite a hitch" Ha Ha

161

Dear Friends at 900 W. Cromer Ave.   9-13-1990

"Soon the ever Falling Leaves will be going their way and that smell of burning will bring out memories we never want to forget" "Squirrels on your fence and for me, "Paper Leaves" from boxes and boxes of great write-ups - News articles - photos - 1945 overseas stuff, old theatre programs and tons of things that pack-rats Keep!

"In The Press" + Wandering Hoosier "leaves are handy + more recent than 1925 or 1932 blurbs! Thanks for helping me stay on the track with so many Hoosier Folks! The best! After the 1923-29 years with Ezra Buzzington's Rube Band of Eaton, In. I had earned a title of Pt. man! For no special reason I always did many interviews with reporters, radio people and loved the intrigue of meeting special folks at special events. I vowed to go into some phase of public relations if I lost fingers + couldn't do the ol' licorice stick; I do believe that a bit of Clarinet work + some letters each day keeps arthritis out" I'm doing a "living room" concert next Tuesday for about twenty here at our assisted living apt. Will use Bass Clar. on "Beautiful

II. Dreamer" – "Amazing Grace". "Flap Tongue Boogie"

I'm sending along my "Stolzhill Work Sheets" I thought the "attic of my mind" would be O.K. to write from but it looks a bit silly! Maybe something interesting is in there! I did dwell on Buzzington and Hoosier recall!

"We hope you are Healthy – Happy n' all the good stuff"

My mail box will hold a lot more – about four or five letters a day goes to many I've never seen! It's great that so many write back! a type of lonesome ness exists. The American Dream is alive and can be seen thru the smoke of the "Burning Leaves"

Do you think at 85 that I'm home–sick?   Ha!!a!

"Christian Love"
Gabe n' Marguerite
Toledo OHIO – 6-30-1928

Marge in wheel chair Broken Pelvis

Wonderful cards on our 62nd

163

Hoosier Hot Shot
COLUMBIA PICTURES
RECORDS

Dear Friends - "a fast, few, cool words
to wish you an enjoyable summer &
good health" 102° for a few days, 68°
today.
I'm busy on music things and it seems
my habit of writing these many years has
become almost like a chain letter. I'm
trying to catch up after getting behind
when Marguerite needed so much!
I just found "She Was a Washout In The
Black out". HaHa - I had forgotten that
War 2 - ditty - So many are wanting photos
& don't realize how expensive 8x10's have
become. As much as 4⁵⁰ each! I can't afford
to order hundreds to get a price! Oh well!
I am wont to think of days back in 1975-82
when I gave photos with album orders!
going for physical to see if I can go to Ind.
for a visit! You n' Jackie have some
fun - lots o' fun! I'll be thinking about
how to act as a great - great grand -
father! HaHa! Some good ol' boys n' girls
keep knocking on my door to visit! I'm
on F. M. Radio Talk shows and still Toot
Still have my own teeth - HaHa!
"Hope you like where you are - with what
you have - doing what you can" - LUV -
Ol' Gabeeto

To Music Man "Anecdotes"   7-24-91
Styaghill -

I bought an alto Sax at the Conn Factory
Elkhart - in 1923 - It was 93º⁰, case in-
cluded- Had snap on pads which was
an innovation at the time. I never had
to replace them and last year a fan
in Fairmount, Ind. gave me 600º⁰ for
it and 200º⁰ for an old H.H.S. drum and
175º⁰ for an old Albert Clarinet that I got
in a Chicago pawn shop for 35º⁰

I traded my Soprano Sax to an L.A.
Collector for 100 albums + 100 tapes
which are all sold now @ 20º⁰ each.
I have 4 albums left - will keep 2 for
posterity! HaHa!
a West German Co. will probably be
doing albums for me soon.
                        Ol' Jabesto

"So, I do get a
few dollars from
my mail & keeps me
going"

1-503-636-7110 –

Hoosier **Hot Shot**
COLUMBIA PICTURES
RECORDS

Sunday Jan 12 - 1992
4 A.M.   40° Nice Rain –
"Can't Sleep."

Dear Friends in Cuyahoga Falls,
"time to recall, reflect and ask how your
move from Muncie has turned out"
"My world presented hectic problems in 1990
1991 and with wonderful aid from family
+ friends, I'm doing better and finding
out what my stay on this great earth is
all about"
With low-interest cutting my income by 60%
I'm still able to do O.K. in my own style!
The interest in Hoosier Hot Shots is being picked
up now by "Baby Boomers" (40's n' 50's) who
want to get my V.C.R's + look at Nostalgia, So
today – I'll do several orders plus some
audio cassettes, plus letters. Busy, busy has a
pretty good "pay off".
Still doing our trusts n' Estate problems. Marge
died Feb. 17th – WOWO-Ft. Wayne did a Memory
program + I was swamped with mail + calls.
I still supply material n' songs there (46 years)
Please send a word along – I did 12 days in
Indiana Oct-Nov. and raked + burnt leaves!
It was beautiful! "Muncie writes to me about
how they miss your writing" – Love – Ol' Gabe

This letter was written two days before Gabe's death. To the
very end he was able to find a reason to be cheerful.

166

Marge died 2-17-1991 -(90 yr old) **Jackie Stodghill**
Gabe died 1-14-1992 (87 yr old)

Dear Gabe,

For days since receiving your letter about Marguerite I've been pondering on what I can say to be of comfort to you. My conclusion is, nothing. The same, "I'm sorry", sounds so trite, but from the heart. Your memories of life with Marguerite are what will become your comfort and biggest treasure when the pain of losing her lessens.

That brings me to my musing over you as a person, dealing with your loss. If ever, and I haven't been abe to think of anyone else I've ever known, who has the capacity to make each day of some value as you have. You don't sit and wait for someone else to bring meaning to your days, you involve yourself in giving value to others life which should leave you with a tremendous sense of fulfillment. And that generally is our contentment. Our contribution to others, in most instances, is the food of our emotional well-being which rules our daily stability. If that need is nutured, what more can we demand? You have always kept busy with your second love, music, it will not forsake you now. How very fortunate you are.

We both know, and I'll keep it a secret even though you don't, you're not a spring chicken, but you sure do keep the hen house of life active with you willingness in making others happy. You're intense need of sharing your music and yourself with others is amazing; the joy you give is genuine and food for the soul to your following, old and new. You are a special person.

You know, I think most women feel, that on a whole women are more capable of making a meaningfull life for themselves after a husbands death than vice versa. I suppose because she has always been the "keeper" of a family and is better versed in a changeable nature from one duty to another at the drop of a hat. Not that she chooses widowhood, but we feel more of a kinsmanship with the world, a mothering of all, forever I guess. But, I see in your situation may be the exception. You have stayed involved with others, it's your nature and will be your biggest consolation.

You're loved and looked to by others for your caring ways. I don't see that likely changing. It will sustain you.

I remain,

Fondly,

Jackie

Gabe - Jackie said it for both of us better than I could have, so I won't try adding to it.

Dick

Jackie's letter to Gabe was written upon hearing of the death of his beloved Marguerite.

UNIVERSITY LIBRARIES   Muncie, Indiana 47306-0160

Mr. Dick Stodghill
1750 4th St.
Cuyahoga Falls, OH 44221-4779

July 26, 2001

Dear Mr. Stodghill:

Allow me to introduce myself: I am a librarian at Ball State University, and when I'm not doing that, I continue to keep up my former life as a classical French horn player. A few months ago, I came across a reissued CD of the Hoosier Hot Shots. I was interested in knowing a bit more about the guys and was surprised to discover that very little has been written about them. So I started digging a bit harder and found your initial column from February 18, 1982 asking, in essence, "What's a Hoosier Hot Shot?" Columns from a few days later suggested that you were flooded with information, more than you ever expected.

I called the library of the Muncie Star Press to see if they had a file on the Hot Shots and/or an index of your columns. The file had just two of your stories and one obituary, all of which I had stumbled on previously. The librarian further reported, with some regret I am happy to say, that the indexes for most editorial columns had been eliminated some time past due to a space crunch. She said that much of the original material had been returned to the authors. Hence, I am writing to ask if you might have kept an index of your columns and/or retained any of the information you received about the Hot Shots that you might be willing to share.

Any information or suggestions you might offer would be gratefully received. Thank you.

Sincerely Yours,

Suzanne Rice

Suzanne Rice
Acting Associate Dean for Library Public Services
Ball State University
Muncie IN 47306

Documents disappear or are destroyed. Soon little remains to tell of our lives, even those of the Hoosier Hot Shots. In a small way this book may help keep the memories alive.

HOT SHOTS MOVIES & SOUNDIES

The Hoosier Hot Shots appeared in 21 movies, no question about that. Gabe thought it was 22 and Ken said there were 23. Could they have been thinking of a Soundie or two? No, they meant real movies. The Hot Shots did make a pair of Soundies, but unless a person under the age of 70 has done some research it is unlikely he or she has any idea of what a Soundie might be. Perhaps that's because it was a very poor choice of names for something that had both sound and a motion picture.

A three-minute performance – the average length of a 78 rpm record - was viewed on a machine called a Panoram. A great many of them were around from 1941 through 1947, then as television hit the scene the Panorams disappeared. They were fine while they lasted, offering anyone who deposited a dime in the slot an opportunity to see their favorite big bands or other performers in action. That included the Hoosier Hot Shots, whose 1942 Soundies "From The Indies To The Andes In His Undies" and "K.P. Serenade" can be found on VHS and perhaps on DVD.

Seventeen of the movies in which the boys made an appearance were Columbia Pictures productions. They were always seen as a quartet with Gil Taylor being the fourth man in all but three. Frank Kettering rounded out the group in *In Old Monterey, Hoosier Holiday* and *National Barn Dance*.

169

Who is this handsome dude? He was a close friend of Gabe Ward and the leading man in eight of the Hoosier Hot Shots movies. A singer by profession, he replaced Frank Sinatra as vocalist in the Tommy Dorsey Orchestra when Sinatra struck out on his own. Then he became a singing cowboy when they were all the rage in Hollywood. His name: Ken Curtis. Those who never heard of Ken might remember him as Festus Haggen in 239 episodes of television's long running Gunsmoke series. C'mon, get serious you say? No kidding, that's him without a scraggly beard, a squint and a drawl. It required some serious acting for him to play the role of Festus. Gabe said a character actor name Shug Fischer and Curtis would hang out together on movie sets and trade lines in funny accents. "It was the beginning of his Festus character," said Gabe. Born in Colorado in 1916, Curtis died in his sleep of a heart attack in 1991.

Gene Autry was the star of *In Old Monterey* and Dale Evans, the future Mrs. Roy Rogers, was the leading lady in *Hoosier Holiday*. In *Rockin' In The Rockies* the Hot Shots teamed up with The Three Stooges while the star of *Hollywood Varieties* was Robert Alda. Comedian Robert Benchley was seen in *National Barn Dance* and Rosemary Lane starred in *Sing Me a Song Of Texas*. Nat King Cole and his trio appeared in *Swing In The Saddle*.

Character actors and singer-actors well known at the time but for the most part forgotten in later years appeared in various films that included the Hot Shots. Chief among them were Guy Kibbee and Noah Berry, Sr. Guinn "Big Boy" Williams was in many of the pictures and others teamed up with the boys included Andy Clyde, Smiley Burnette, Gabby Hayes, Slim Summerville, Pat Buttram, and Jay Silverheels, best remembered as Tonto, "the masked man's faithful Indian companion" in *The Lone Ranger* TV series.

Along with a few of those mentioned above, the many singers and vocal groups of the day seen in those Hot Shots films included Bob Wills, Spade Cooley, Merle Travis, Jack Leonard, Stuart Hamblen, Jimmy Wakely, Pinky Tomlin, Lulu Belle and Scotty, The Pied Pipers, The Dinning Sisters, The De Castro Sisters, Riders of the Purple Sage, Art West and His Sunset Riders, and Hal McIntyre and His Orchestra.

The majority of the Columbia films, but not all, were directed by Ray Nazarro.

The 21 known movies, release dates and studios in which the Hoosier Hot Shots made music and did a bit of acting were:

In Old Monterey (Aug 14, 1939 - Republic)
Hoosier Holiday (Sep 15, 1943 -Republic)
Swing In The Saddle (Jul 3, 1944 - Columbia)
The National Barn Dance (Sep 5, 1944 - Paramount)
Sing Me A Song Of Texas (Feb 8, 1945 - Columbia)
Rockin' In The Rockies (Apr 17 1945 - Columbia)
Rhythm Round-Up (Jun 7, 1945 - Columbia)
Song Of The Prairie (Sep 27 1945 - Columbia)
Throw A Saddle On A Star (Mar 14 1946 - Columbia)
That Texas Jamboree (May 16, 1946 - Columbia)
Cowboy Blues (Jul 8, 1946 - Columbia)
Singing On The Trail (Sep 2, 1946 - Columbia)
Lone Star Moonlight (Dec 12 1946 - Columbia)
Over The Santa Fe Trail (Feb 13 1947 - Columbia)
Swing The Western Way (Jun 26, 1947 - Columbia)
Smoky River Serenade (Aug 21, 1947 - Columbia)
Rose Of Santa Rosa (Jan 2, 1948 - Columbia)
Song Of Idaho (Mar 30, 1948 - Columbia)
Singing Spurs (Sep 22, 1948 - Columbia)

The Arkansas Swing May 1, 1949 - Columbia)
Hollywood Varieties (Jan 14, 1950 - Lippert)

The March 13, 1937 issue of Prairie Farmer magazine reported that the Hoosier Hot Shots would appear in a movie called *Mountain Music*, a film starring comedians Bob Burns and Martha Raye. They are not listed in the film's credits.

Proof that the Hot Shots did not appear in *Mountain Music* came in this quote in a *Hollywood Showdown* column by Evans Plummer: "If you ask Gabe Ward and his fellow Hoosier Hot Shots – Hezzie, Ken and Frank – of Uncle Ezra and National Barn Dance fame, who were here for their first time to appear in Gene Autry's new Republic picture *In Old Montery* . . . "

The songs performed by the Hoosier Hot Shots in movies are documented in some cases, unclear or just unknown in others. The majority of those that are recorded are Hot Shot standards also heard on phonograph records. These include:
She Broke My Heart In Three Places, Dude Cowboy, (Swing In The Saddle); From The Indies To The Andes In his Undies, This Is The Chorus, Swing Little Indians Swing (The National Barn Dance).

Them Hill-Billies Are Mountain Williams Now (Sing Me A Song Of Texas); *That's What I Learned In College* (Rhythm Round-Up); *Wah Hoo!, Wabash Blues, Skee Dee Waddle Dee Waddle Do, Ever So Quiet* (Rockin' In The Rockies); *The Covered Wagon Rolled Right Along, No Romance In Your Soul* (Song Of The Prairie); *The Dummy Song, He's A Hillbilly Gaucho* (Throw A Saddle On A Star); *Somedays You Can't Make a Nickel* (That Texas Jamboree).

The First Thing I Do Every Morning, Since We Put A Radio Out In The Hen House, The Coat And Pants Do All The Work (Cowboy Blues); *When Johnny Brings Lelahani Home* (Lone Star Moonlight); *When Grown Up Ladies Act Like Babies, My Bonnie* (Singing On The Trail); *My Wife Is On A Diet, When You're Smiling* (Swing The Western Way); *Ferdinand The Bull* (Rose Of Santa Rosa); *When Lightnin' Struck The Coon Creek Party Line, The Cheer Parade* (Song Of Idaho); *My Bonnie* (Hollywood Varieties).

Songs in Hot Shots films that they apparently didn't record on 78s but were later issued on LPs or CDs include: *Washboard Stomp, Hey Mabel, Wait At The Gate For Me Katy, On The West Side Of Chicago, and Which Came First The Chicken Or The Egg.*

The above list should not be taken as gospel because the credits for a number of movies either did not list songs or did not attribute them to specific artists.

In a newspaper interview, Gabe Ward had this to say about their film careers: "Those so called action movies paid handsomely. The budget for most of our movies was about $400,000 and we'd have about a ten-day shooting schedule. The Hoosier Hot Shots had a deal with Columbia Pictures for four movies a year. We split $17,500 four ways per movie over a five year contract. We must've made twenty of them, plus a few shorts."

Information on Hoosier Hot Shots movies, including casts, lobby cards and much more can be found online at the Hoosier Hot Shots Museum, a not-to-be-missed site for anyone interested in the boys. Many of the movies can be ordered there through a link to hezzie.com.

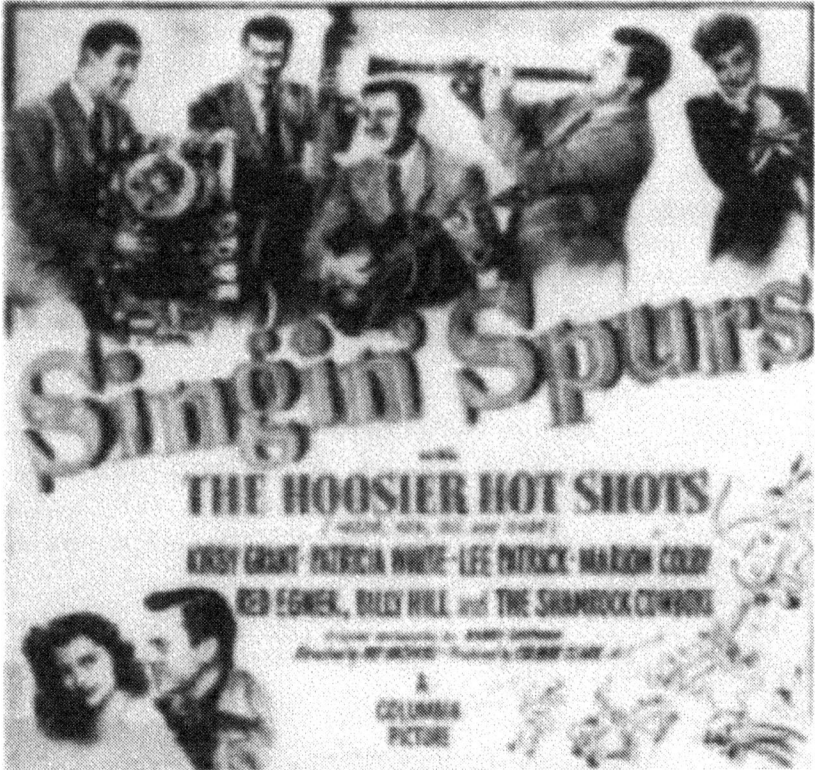

HOOSIER HOT SHOTS CHARTED HITS

Looking over the number of Hoosier Hot Shots recordings to make the Billboard charts can be deceptive. It wasn't until 1944 that Billboard even had a chart for Country & Western music. Some of the groups earlier recordings would certainly have made the chart had it existed because four of them were found on the Popular Music list. While the Hot Shots sold more than three million records – a tremendous number in the era of 78 rpm. discs – much of their popularity could be traced to live radio broadcasts and songs played on a jukebox.

POP CHART LISTINGS:

Date	Top Pos.	Weeks	Title
9-18-37	13	2	*Breezin' Along With The Breeze*
11-19-38	12	1	*Red Hot Fannie*
12-17-38	11	2	*The Man With The Whiskers*
4-01-39	15	1	*Annabelle*
6- ?-44	21	1	* *She Broke My Heart In Three Places*
2-09-46	12	1	*Someday* (You'll Want Me To . . .)

COUNTRY CHART LISTINGS:

Date	Top Pos.	Weeks	Title
6-44	3	2	*She Broke My Heart In Three Places*
1-46	3	10	*Someday* (You'll Want Me To Want You)
2-46	2	16	*Sioux City Sue*

* Joel Whitburn's Pop Memories 1890-1954 does not list this as appearing on the Pop Charts by the HHS or anyone else.
Breezin' Along With The Breeze was a revival of a No. 1 hit by Johnny Marvin in 1926. Other hits recordings at that time were by the Abe Lyman Orchestra and The Revelers.
Red Hot Fannie was a HHS original.
The Man With The Whiskers was a HHS original.
Annabelle was also a Lawrence Welk hit in 1939.
Someday was a 1949 hit by Vaughn Monroe and the Mills Brothers.

Sioux City Sue was a Pop Chart hit by Bing Crosby, Dick Thomas and Tony Pastor.

Guest vocalists on HHS charted hits were:
Annabelle: Skip Farrell
Sioux City Sue: Dick "Two-Ton" Baker

Gabe Ward didn't think much of *Breezin' Along With The Breese*. The song itself was fine, but he felt their recording was out of tune and just bad in general. "I don't see why they didn't release a better copy," he said.

Little is known of Charles "Skip" Farrell, the vocalist on many Hoosier Hot Shots recordings. He was born October 9, 1918 in Illinois, died May 8, 1962 in California. By no means could he be considered a country music vocalist although his pleasant voice was heard on at least a dozen Hot Shots records. Chances are he was a professional singer in Chicago, perhaps with a band or on station WLS, and that led to his teaming up with the boys. Those appear to be his only recordings as he is not listed in the volumes of either Brian Rust or Joel Whitburn.

Sally Foster, a Wisconsin girl who preferred singing the "sweet, old-fashioned songs," is credited by some sources, including Whitburn, as being the vocalist on *Someday*. She wasn't, it was Gil Taylor. Sally was a regular performer on the National Barn Dance.

SALLY FOSTER

Dick "Two-Ton" Baker was a popular figure on Chicago radio for nearly four decades. He recorded on the Mercury label but ironically his biggest hit came on a Decca disc and the Hot Shots received top billing, not Baker. He was born in 1916 and died in 1975. At 6'2" and 350 pounds he lived up to his Two-Ton name. All he ever wanted, he said, was to "play the piano and sing on radio." He got to do both, but he doesn't seem to have appeared on the National Barn Dance. So many people did so over the years, however, that it's more than possible Two-Ton was among them at one time or another.

HOOSIER HOT SHOTS DISCOGRAPHY

Although every known source has been checked, a limited amount of information is available on Hoosier Hot Shots recordings so what follows should not be taken as gospel. It is possible, however, that it is complete. Much of it came from Gabe Ward. He also said there is a discography listing more than 300 HHS recordings at the Library of Congress but I have never been able to find it. Two recordings I'm sure are missing from the following are *The Young-uns Of The Martins and The Coys* and *Then I'll Be Crying For You.* Gabe sent me copies.

Gabe also sent a tape of the first two Hot Shots recordings made in 1932. Unfortunately he did not say where the records were cut, nor did he say if they were ever released to the public or were merely for promotional purposes. It is likely that they were made at the Gennett studio in Richmond. Gennett had stopped making records under its own label but was still doing some recordings for other companies in 1932. *The Cheer Parade* begins with Ken saying the line that would become so familiar: "Are you ready, Hezzie." Ken was still playing the tuba during that first session and was very prominent – or loud – on *Virginia Blues*.

The best discography up to this time contains errors such as listing four songs recorded on March 1, 1939 as having been recorded on that date a year later. The same error appears on a CD. The error is confirmed by two things: the song Annabelle made the pop charts in 1939 and the Vocalion label numbers are obviously out of order. Even so, the discography on the Hoosier Hot Shots Museum website provides a wealth of information concerning which songs could be found on what labels.

For the sake of simplicity and space limitations, where possible only the Vocalion numbers are given here prior to 1944 as it was the lone company to issue nearly all Hot Shots recordings. Beginning with 1944 Decca numbers are used in most cases.

In his outstanding book, *American Premium Record Guide 1900-1965,* Les Docks lists 71 records by the Hoosier Hot Shots. Because so many were issued, all are valued from $5 to $10 on the open market or at auctions. In some cases, Docks says, Melotone 1300 series recordings might bring slightly more. He notes that many HHS songs were issued contemporaneously on Banner, Conqueror, Melotone, Oriole, Perfect, Romeo and Vocalion labels.

Much of what is listed here is taken from a handwritten list given to me by Gabe and unlike most discographies is in chronological rather than alphabetical order. This makes it easy to see the rise and fall of the group's popularity. A number of songs were recorded two or more times, others were issued only as part of an LP record. Many recordings were reissued, frequently on different labels. Vocalion numbers were often the same as those on Okeh records.

The vast majority of the songs were issued on 78 r.p.m. records; those on 45 are so listed below. In later years many were reissued on LPs and CDs. If the label is not known the matrix number is given in parentheses preceded by a question mark. Songs that were recorded but not released are listed separately by matrix number following the year-by-year. Some, as noted, were later issued on LPs and CDs. The recording company abbreviations, most of which do not appear here, are:

Ban – Banner
Bru – Brunswick
Cam – Cameo
Cas – Cameous (45)
Col – Columbia
Con – Conqueror
Cor – Coral
Dec – Decca
Imp – Imperial
JC – J.C. (45)
Kri – Kristal

Mel – Melotone
Oke – Okeh
Ori – Oriole
Oro – Oroco (45)
Per – Perfect
Rex – Rex
Rom – Romeo
Top – Tops (78 & 45)
Tri – Trianon (45)
V – V-Disc
Voc – Vocalion

1932

The Cheer Parade	?	? }
Virgina Blues		}

1934

Farmer Gray	11-13 Voc 3726
Four Thousand Years Ago	11-13 Voc 3724
Hoosier Stomp	11-13 Voc 3725
I'm Looking For A Girl	11-13 Voc 3727
Oakville Twister	11-13 Voc 3725
Sentimental Gentleman From Georgia	11-13 Voc 3726
Whistlin' Joe From Kokomo	11-13 Voc 3724
Yes She Do – No She Don't	11-13 Voc 3727

1935

Back In Indiana	6-14 Voc 3730
Black Eyed Susan Brown	6-14 Voc 3730
Down In The Valley	6-14 Voc 3729
Ha-Cha-Nan	6-14 Voc 3728
I Wish That I Was Back In Indiana	6-14 Col 20291
Meet Me By The Ice House Lizzie	6-14 Voc 3729
This Is The Chorus	6-14 Voc 3728

Bow-Wow Blues	10-28 Voc	3733
Everybody Stomp	10-28 Voc	3742
I Can't Give You Anything But Love	10-28 Voc	5013
Limehouse Blues	10-28 Con	8601
San	10-28 Voc	3731
Them Hill-Billies Are Mountain Williams Now	10-28 oc	3731
Virginia Blues	10-28 Voc	3949
At The Old Maid's Ball	11-02 Con	8615
I Like Bananas Because They Have No Bones	11-2 Voc	3732
Ida	11-02 Voc	3732
They Go Wild, Simply Wild Over Me	11-02 Con	8615
Where Are You Going Honey	11-02 Voc	3735

1936

At The Darktown Strutter's Ball	2-26 Voc	3734
I Like Mountain Music	2-26 Voc	3853
Nobody's Sweetheart	2-26 Voc	3734
Wah-Hoo	2-26 Voc	3733
You're Driving Me Crazy (What Did I Do)	2-26 Voc	3739
Hold 'Er Eb'ner	3-30 Voc	3737
Ain't She Sweet	6-15 Col	C1405
Bye Bye Blues	6-15 Con	8745
I Wish I Could Shimmy Like My Sister Kate	6-15 Voc	3644
I'll Soon Be Rolling Home	6-15 Voc	3740
Is It True What They Say About Dixie	6-15 Voc	3735
It Ain't Nobody's Biz'ness What I Do	6-15 Voc	3901
No More	6-15 Voc	3901
Some Of These Days	6-15 Voc	3737
Take Me Out To The Ball Game	6-15 Voc	3736
Alexander's Ragtime Band	10-05 Voc	3741
Hot Lips	10-05 Voc	3744
Margie	10-05 Voc	3741
Shake Your Dogs	10-05 Voc	3738
Sweet Sue, Just You	10-05 Voc	3744
That's What I Learned In College	10-05 Voc	3738
Toot, Toot, Tootsie	10-05 Voc	3739
Jingle Bells	11-17 Voc	3740

182

1937

Breezin' Along With the Breeze	1-20	Voc	3644
I Ain't Got Nobody	1-20	Voc	3949
Pick That Bass	1-20	Voc	3742
The Coat and the Pants Do All Of The Work	1-20	Voc	3743
I Want A Girl	1-21	Voc	3853
I've Got A Bimbo Down On The Bamboo Isle	1-21	Voc	3745
Goofus	1-29	Voc	3683
Runnin' Wild	1-29	Voc	3683
When You Wore A Tulip	1-29	Voc	3743

1938

Down Home Rag	2-15	Voc	4090
Etiquette Blues	2-15	Voc	4024
Farewell Blues	2-15	Voc	4024
Meet Me Tonight In The Cow Shed	2-15	Voc	4090
After You've Gone	3-01	Voc	4215
Tit Willow	3-01	Voc	4481
How Ya Gonna Keep 'Em Down On The Farm	6-06	Voc	4352
Milenberg Joys	6-06	Voc	4352
Oh By Jingo!	6-06	Voc	4614
Red Hot Fannie	6-06	Voc	4289
Swinging With Dora	6-06	Voc	4289
Wabash Blues	6-06	Voc	4614
You Said Something When You Said Dixie	6-06	Voc	4215
A Hot Dog A Blanket And You	9-14	Voc	4426
The Flat Foot Floogee	9-14	Voc	4426
The Sheik Of Araby	9-14	Voc	4481
The Girl Friend Of The Whirling Dervish	10-28	Voc	C2369
The Man With The Whiskers	10-28	Voc	4502
Ferdinand The Bull	11-15	Voc	4554
When Paw Was Courtin' Maw	11-15	Voc	4554

1939

Skeede-Waddle-Dee-Waddle-Do	?	Voc	4893
Like A Monkey Likes Coconuts	2-02	Voc	4688
When You're Smiling	2-02	Voc	4893
Where Has My Little Dog Gone	2-02	Voc	4688
Annabelle	3-01	Voc	4697
Avalon	3-01	Voc	4823
Ever So Quiet	3-01	Voc	4824
It's A Lonely Trail	3-01	Voc	4697
From The Indies To The Andes In His Undies	4-22	Voc	4696
Beer Barrel Polka	5-10	Voc	4824
Three Little Fishies	5-10	Voc	4823
Look On The Bright Side	5-11	Voc	5013
Rural Rhythm	9-14	Voc	5214
The Martins And The Coys	9-14	Voc	5214
The Merry Go Roundup	9-14	Voc	5119
Willie, Willie, Will Ya!	9-14	Voc	5119
Are You Havin' Any Fun	9-21	Voc	5145
Put On Your Old Red Flannels	9-21	Voc	5132
Sam The College Leader Man	9-21	Voc	5132
Start The Day Right	9-21	Voc	5145
He'd Have To Get Under, Get Out And Get Under	12-08	Voc	5345
Oh You Beautiful Doll	12-08	Voc	5345
Okay Baby	12-08	Voc	5809
The Pants That My Pappy Gave To Me	12-08	Voc	5485
Careless	12-12	Voc	5295
Connie's Got Connections In Connecticut	12-12	Voc	5437
In An Old Dutch Garden	12-12	Voc	5295

1940

Everything I Do, I Sure Do Fine	1-09	Voc	5584
I Don't Care (Life's a Jamboree)	1-09	Voc	5584
Shirley	1-09	Voc	5622
What Is So Rare	1-09	Voc	5485
Big Noise From Kokomo	1-29	Voc	5754
I'm Just Wild About Harry	1-29	Voc	5390

Ma She's Making Eyes at Me	1-29	Voc	5390
Swanee	1-29	Voc	5437
Moving Day In Jungle Town	2-02	Voc	4946
No, No, Nora	4-11	Voc	5547
O-HI-O	4-11	Voc	5547
Phil The Fluter's Ball	4-11	Voc	5622
Who's Sorry Now	4-11	Voc	5754
Diga Diga Do	6-14	Voc	5665
Kitten With The Big Green Eye	6-14	Voc	5665
My Wife Is On A Diet	6-14	Voc	5708
Poor Papa	6-14	Voc	5708
Everybody Loves My Baby	8-06	Voc	6017
The Guy Who Stole My Wife	8-06	Voc	6217
The Poor Little Country Maid	8-06	Voc	5809
Tiger Rag	8-06	Voc	6017
Beatrice Fairfax, Tell Me What To Do	10-02	Voc	5853
I Just Wanna Play With You	10-02	Voc	5942
Noah's Wife	10-02	Voc	5891
St. Louis Blues	10-02	Voc	6217
That's Where I Meet My Girl	10-02	Voc	5942
Way Down In Arkansaw	10-02	Voc	5891
When There's Tears In The Eyes Of A Potato	10-02	Voc	5853

1941

Keep An Eye On Your Heart	1-22	Voc	6065
Let's Not And Say We Did	1-22	Voc	6114
Swing Little Indians, Swing	1-22	Voc	6173
With A Twist Of The Wrist	1-22	Voc	6065
Dude Cowboy	1-27	Voc	6503
The Streets Of New York	1-27	Voc	6173
There'll Be Some Changes Made	1-27	Voc	6114
He's A Hillbilly Gaucho	6-05	Voc	6348
Lazy River	6-05	Con	9918
Since We Put A Radio Out In The Hen House	6-05	Voc	6425
The Band Played On	6-05	Voc	6273
Windmill Tillie	6-05	Voc	6348
Blues (My Naughty Baby Gives To Me)	6-09	Voc	6599
Bull Frog Serenade	6-09	Voc	6503

Rhyme Your Sweetheart	6-09	Voc	6599
The Hut-Sut Song	6-09	Voc	6273
When Lightnin' Struck The Coon Creek			
Party Line	6-09	Voc	6425
No Romance In Your Soul	6-15	Con	9918

1942

She Was A Washout In The Blackout	1-23	Voc	6613
She's Got A Great Big Army Of Friends	1-23	Voc	6613
They Go Goo Goo, Gaga, Goofy Over Gobs	1-23	?(C4160)	

1943

No Recordings

1944

Don't Change Horses	3-?	Dec	4442
She Broke My Heart In Three Places	3-?	Dec	4442
Bringin' Home The Bacon From Macon	9-18	Cor	64000
Dummy Song	9-18	Dec	4455
Some Days You Can't Make A Nickel	9-18	Dec	4455
Them Hillbillies Are Mountain Williams Now	9-18	Dec	46023
You Kissed Me Once	9-18	Dec	46062
The Barn Dance Polka	11-?	Dec	4453
This Is The Chorus	11-?	Dec	4453

1945

From The Indies To The Andes In His Undies	1-17	Cor	64000
The Musket Came Down From The Door	1-17	Dec	46062
*Is It True What They Say About Dixie	2-?-45	V	VP 1275
*Sentimental Gentleman From Georgia	2-?-45	V	VP 1275
Sioux City Sue	10-?	Dec	18745
Someday (You'll Want Me To Want You)	10-?	Dec	18738
There's A Tear In My Beer Tonight	10-?	Dec	18745
You Two-Timed Me One Time Too Often	10-?	Dec	18738

* V-Discs recorded for the military

1946

The First Thing I Do Every Morning	5-07	Dec	46020
When Johnny Brings Lelahani Home	5-07	Dec	46020
Divorce Me C.O.D.	10-?	Dec	46023

1953

When Grown Up Ladies Act Like Babies	3-?	Oro	?
Foolin's Fun	9-?	Oro	?
Indiana Corn-certo No. 1	?	Tri	TR121
The Onion Song	?	Tri	TR121

1957

Daniel Boone	?	Cas	45-C105
Humming Bird	?	Top	R-261
The Kentuckian	?	Top	R-261
The Man From Laramie	?	Cas	45-C105

1960

Jingle Bells	5-12	JC	102
The Man With The Whiskers	5-12	JC	102

RECORDED BUT NOT RELEASED

		Matrix
Shake Your Feet	6-14-35	C1005
You May Belong To Somebody Else But I Love You Just the Same	6-14-35	C1000
Jam Making Time	11-02-35	C1164
Stay Out Of The South	2-26-36	?
Ah Woo! Ah Woo! To You	8-03-36	C1444
*Back Home Again In Indiana	1-20-37	C1756
Kid In The Three Cornered Pants	11-21-37	C1759
*Down In Jungle Town	9-14-38	C2315
Toy Town Jamboree	11-15-38	C2386
There Are Just Two I's In Dixie	12-21-39	WC2856
How Come You Do Me Like You Do	10-02-40	WC3347
*My Bonnie	1-27-41	C3582
Tavern In The Town	6-04-41	C3863
*Cuddle Up A Little Closer	1-20-42	C4157
My Little Girl	1-20-42	C4161
*One Eyed Sam	1-20-42	C4155
*The Covered Wagon Rolled Right Along	1-20-42	C4159
*You'd Be Surprised	1-20-42	C4162

  * Later released on Compact Discs

V-Discs recorded in February 1945 but not released:

The Berries and the Buttercups	VP 1198
Phil the Fluter's Ball	VP 1198
She Broke My Heart In Three Places	VP 1403
Down In the Valley	VP 1403
All Girl Medley	?
*Down In the Valley	VP 1403
*Tiger Rag	VP 1403

  * Erroneously listed as by Spike Jones & His City Slickers.

LP (Long Play) RECORDS

Hoosier Hot Shots -Tops Records L1541 (Recorded in **1957** with the three original Hot Shots plus Gil Taylor))
There's No Romance In Your Soul
My Blue Heaven
Wah-Hoo
Hound Dog
Meet Me By The Ice House Lizzie
I Like Bananas Because They Have No Bones
Tiger Rag
After I Say I'm Sorry
Them Hill-Billies Are Mountain Williams Now
Mister Sandman
Someday
Toot, Toot, Tootsie

Hoosier Hot Shots – HHS Records HHS 100 (Recorded in **1962** with the three original Hot Shots plus Nate Harrison and Keith Milheim.)
Sweet Georgia Brown
Ida
Marianne
The Darktown Strutters Ball
Toot, Toot, Tootsie
Washboard Stomp
Down By The Riverside
Indian Love Call
Heartaches
Wabash Charleston

The Original Hoosier Hot Shots – Dot Records DLP 25561 (This was a **1964** re-release of HHS 100. Also released as a 7-inch version for jukeboxes that included: Sweet Georgia Brown: Marianne: Toot, Toot, Tootsie; Down By The Riverside; The Darktown Strutters Ball; Heartaches.)

**Are You Ready Hezzie? The Original Hoosier Hot Shots –
Dot Records DLP 25694** (This was a **1966** release with the
three original Hot Shots plus Nate Harrison and Keith Milheim
A monaural version was issued as # 3694.)
From the Indies To The Andes In His Undies
Lonesome Road
He's Got The Whole World In His Hands
Autumn Leaves
Meet Me By The Ice House Lizzie
I Like Bananas Because They Have No Bones
Jingle Bells
Everyone's Hometown
Hometown Brass Medley: Show Boy; Goodnight Irene; Smiles
Hometown Rag Medley: Tiger Rag; Wabash Blues

**Are You Ready Hezzie, The Hoosier Hot Shots – Sandy
Hook Records 86.** This LP was made from original 78 r.p.m.
recordings.
At The Darktown Strutters Ball
Nobody's Sweetheart
Ha-Cha-Nan
Ida
This Is The Chorus
Margie
Annabelle
Bye Bye Blues
I Like Mountain Music
Some Of These Days
It Ain't Nobody's Biz'ness What I Do
Hold 'Er Eb'ner
Take Me Out To The Ball Game
It's A Lonely Trail
Barn Dance Polka
Farewell Blues

The Hoosier Hot Shots! – Mary Ann Records HHS 937
A reissued collection of original 78 r.p.m records.
Alexander's Ragtime Band
Darktown Strutters Ball
I've Got A Bimbo Down On The Bamboo Isle
Runnin' Wild
Nobody's Sweetheart
Meet Me Tonight In The Cow Shed
Toot, Toot, Tootsie
Wah Hoo!
Pretty Baby
Oh, How She Lied
When You Wore A Tulip
Sweet Jenny Lee
Is It True What They Say About Dixie
Some Of These Days

Hoosier Hot Shots 1935-1938 – Sunbeam Records MFC-C10. A collection of original 78 r.p.m. recordings reissued in **1983**. The title is misleading as some of the recordings were made after 1938.
At The Darktown Strutters Ball
Nobody's Sweetheart
Ha-Cha-Nan
Ida
This Is The Chorus
Margie
Annabelle
Bye Bye Blues
I Like Mountain Music
Some Of These Days
It Ain't Nobody's Biz'ness What I Do
Hold 'Er Eb'ner
Take Me Out To The Ball Game
It's A Lonely Trail
Barn Dance Polka
Farewell Blues

Judy Canova/Hoosier Hot Shots – Hurrah Records H-1051
HHS songs reissued from Tops Records L1541. Only HHS
songs listed.
There's No Romance In Your Soul
Meet Me By The Ice House Lizzie
Them Hill-Billies Are Mountain Williams Now
I Like Bananas Because They Have No Bones
Mister Sandman

Wah Hoo! – Golden Tone Records C4060
A reissue of Tops Records L1541

**The Hoosier Hot Shots Sing Hound Dog And Other
Favorites – Viking VK 804**
This LP contained only five HHS recordings from Tops
Records L1541 with the rest by another group.
Hound Dog
Them Hill-Billies Are Mountain Williams Now
Mister Sandman
There's No Romance In Your Soul
Meet Me By The Ice House Lizzie

Original Hoosier Hot Shots – Mark 56 Records
Released in 1982, this LP produced by Ken Trietsch consists of
two Mutual Radio HHS broadcasts.

**Nashville's Original Hoosier Hot Shots Country Kiddin' –
Spinorama M-162**
Both inside and out, this is a travesty, a testament to careless,
sloppy writing and editing. The Hoosier Hot Shots had no
connection whatsoever to Nashville, nor did radio station WLS.
According to the cover the station broadcast from that city in
Tennessee rather than Chicago, its home since 1924. Amazing.
One of the ten songs on the LP, Hogwash, was not recorded by
the HHS. Those that were are taken from Tops Records L1541.
There's No Romance In Your Soul
Hound Dog
Them Hill-Billies Are Mountain Williams Now
Mister Sandman

Meet Me By the Ice House Lizzie
Someday
I like Bananas Because They Have No Bones
Wah Hoo!

Hoosier Hot Shots Live – Amalgamated 142
Does this recording actually exist? Probably.

Unfortunately none of the Hoosier Hot Shots LPs listed here are in print at the time of this writing. Some might be found used either online, in book and record stores or at flea markets.

CD (Compact Disc) RECORDINGS

At the time of this writing all of the following CDs other than the first one listed are available from www.hezzie.com or from a wonderful website for those who enjoy the Hoosier Hot Shots: www.hoosierhotshots.com. This writer recommends the latter site as it critiques each CD as well as offering a storehouse of other information. To order CDs it will direct the reader to the Hezzie site.

Hoosier Hot Shots Rural Rhythm 1935-1942 –
Columbia/Legacy Records CK 52735. Issued in 1992. Out of Print at the time of this writing.
San
I like Bananas Because They Have No Bones
Sweet Sue
Connie's Got Connections In Connecticut
Rural Rhythm
The Girl Friend Of The Whirling Dervish
Everybody Stomp
It Ain't Nobody's Biz'ness What I Do
That's Where I Meet My Girl
Goofus
From The Indies To The Andes In His Undies

What Is So Rare
The Coat And The Pants Do All The Work
She's Got A Great Big Army Of Friends
My Bonnie
Noah's Wife
One-Eyed Sam
I Just Wanna Play With You
Like A Monkey Likes Coconuts
Moving Day In Jungle Town

Hoosier Hot Shots "Are You Ready Hezzie" – Circle Records CCD-905. Issued in 1993.
I Like Mountain Music
My Blue Heaven
Wah Hoo
After I Say I'm Sorry
The Coat And The Pants Do All Of The Work
Sweet Jennie Lee
Pretty Baby
My Little Bimbo Down On The Bamboo Isle
Toot, Toot, Tootsie
Some Days You Can't Make a Nickel
Breezin' Along With The Breeze
Meet Me Tonight In The Cow Shed
Texas Blues
What's The Good Word Mr. Bluebird
Skeleton Rag
Put On Your Slippers And Fill Up Your Pipe
Someday
I Like Bananas Because They Have No Bones
When You Wore A Tulip
Since We Put The Radio Out In The Hen House
Cuddle Up A Little Closer
Beer Barrel Polka
Nobody's Sweetheart
That's What I Learned In College
Runnin' Wild

Hoosier Hot Shots In Order #1 (1934-35) Sagamore Records #251. Issued in 2002.
Sentimental Gentleman From Georgia
Hoosier Stomp
Yes She Do – No She Don't
Whistlin' Joe From Kokomo
Four Thousand Years Ago
Farmer Gray
Oakville Twister
I'm Looking For A Girl
Black Eyed Susan Brown
This Is The Chorus
Down In The Valley
Ha-Cha-Nan
Meet Me By The Ice House Lizzie
Back In Indiana
Limehouse Blues
I Can't Give You Anything But Love
San
Everybody Stomp
Bow Wow Blues
Them Hill-Billies Are Mountain Williams Now
Virginia Blues
I Like Bananas Because They Have No Bones

Hoosier Hot Shots In Order #2 (1935-36) Sagamore Records #252. Issued in 2002.
Ida
Where Are You Going, Honey
They Go Wild, Simply Wild Over Me
At The Old Maids Ball
Wah Hoo
At The Darktown Strutters Ball
Nobody's Sweetheart
I Like Mountain Music
You're Driving Me Crazy
Hold 'Er Eb'ner
Take Me Out To The Ball Game
Bye Bye Blues

I'll Soon Be Rolling Home
Ain't She Sweet
Is It True What They Say About Dixie
I Wish I Could Shimmy Like My Sister Kate
It Ain't Nobody's Biz'ness What I Do
No More
Some Of These Days
That's What I Learned In College
Margie
Alexander's Ragtime Band

Hoosier Hot Shots In Order #3 (1936-38) Sagamore Records #253. Issued in 2002.
Hot Lips
Shake Your Dogs
Sweet Sue
Toot, Toot, Tootsie
Jingle Bells
Pick That Bass
I Ain't Got Nobody
The Coat And The Pants Do All Of The Work
Breezin' Along With The Breeze
I Want A Girl
I've Got A Bimbo Down On The Bamboo Isle
Goofus
When You Wore A Tulip
Runnin' Wild
Farewell Blues
Down Home Rag
Meet Me Tonight In The Cow Shed
Etiquette Blues
After You've Gone
Tit Willow
Oh By Jingo!
You Said Something When You Said Dixie

Hoosier Hot Shots In Order #4 (1938-39)   Sagamore Records #254. Issued in 2002.

How Ya Gonna Keep 'Em Down On The Farm
Red Hot Fannie
Swinging With Dora
Milenberg Joys
Wabash Blues
The Shiek Of Araby
A Hot Dog A Blanket And You
The Flat Foot Floogee
The Man With The Whiskers
The Girl Friend of the Whirling Dervish
When Paw Was Courtin' Maw
Ferdinand The Bull
Skeede-Waddle-Dee-Waddle-Do
Where Has My Little Dog Gone
When You're Smiling
Like A Monkey Likes Coconuts
From The Indies To The Andes In His Undies
Three Little Fishies
Beer Barrel Polka
Look On The Bright Side
The Merry Go Roundup

Hoosier Hot Shots In Order #5 (1939-40) Sagamore Records #255. Issued in 2002.

Willie, Willie Will Ya!
The Martins And The Coys
Rural Rhythm
Start The Day Right
Are You Havin' Any Fun
Put On Your Old Red Flannels
Sam The College Leader Man
The Pants That My Pappy Gave To Me
He'd Have To Get Under, Get Out And Get Under
Oh, You Beautiful Doll
Okay Baby
Careless
In An Old Dutch Garden

Connie's Got Connections In Connecticut
Everything I Do, I Sure Do Fine
What Is So Rare
I Don't Care (Life's A Jamboree)
Shirley
Big Noise From Kokomo
Ma, She's Making Eyes At Me
Swanee
I'm Just Wild About Harry

Hoosier Hot Shots In Order #6 (1940) Sagamore Records #256. Issue in 2002.
Moving Day In Jungle Town
Annabelle
Avalon
It's A Lonely Trail
Ever So Quiet
Who's Sorry Now
No, No Nora
O-Hi-O
Phil The Fluters Ball
My Wife Is On A Diet
Diga Diga Do
Poor Papa
Kitten With The Big Green Eyes
Everybody Loves My Baby
The Guy Who Stole My Wife
Poor Little Country Maid
Tiger Rag
Noah's Wife
Way Down In Arkansas
That's Where I Meet My Girl
I Just Wanna Play With You
When There's Tears In The Eyes Of A Potato

Hoosier Hot Shots In Order #7 (1940-41) Sagamore Records #257. Issued in 2002.
Beatrice Fairfax, Tell Me What To Do
St. Louis Blues
Keep An Eye On Your Heart
With A Twist Of The Wrist
Let's Not And Say We Did
Swing Little Indians, Swing
There'll Be Some Changes Made
Dude Cowboy
The Streets Of New York
No Romance In Your Soul
Windmill Tillie
The Band Played On
Since We Put A Radio Out In The Henhouse
He's A Hillbilly Gaucho
Lazy River
Rhyme Your Sweetheart
Bull Frog Serenade
Blues (My Naughty Baby Gives To Me)
When Lightnin' Struck The Coon Creek Party Line
The Hut-Sut Song

Hoosier Hot Shots In Order #8 (1944-57) Sagamore Records #258. Issued in 2002.
She Broke My Heart In Three Places
Don't Change Horses
This Is The Chorus
The Barn Dance Polka
The Musket Came Down From The Door
Dummy Song
Them Hillbillies Are Mountain Williams Now
You Kissed Me Once
Somedays You Can't Make A Nickel
Bringin' Home The Bacon
From The Indies To The Andes In His Undies
You Two Timed Me One Time Too Often
Sioux City Sue
Someday **(Error. A repeat of Somedays You Can't ...)**

199

There's A Tear In My Beer Tonight
The First Thing I Do Every Morning
When Johnny Brings Lelahani Home
Divorce Me C.O.D.
Indiana Corn-certo #1
The Onion Song
Foolin's Fun
When The Grownup Ladies Act Like Babies
Daniel Boone
Humming Bird
The Kentuckian
The Man From Laramie
The Man With The Whiskers
Jingle Bells

The preceding eight Sagamore CDs are also available as a complete set.

The Definitive Hoosier Hot Shots Collection – Collector's Choice Music CCM 378-2. Issued 2003. Two CD set. **CD#1**:
Meet Me By The Ice House Lizzie
Them Hillbillies Are Mountain Williams Now
I Like Bananas Because They Have No Bones
Wah-Hoo!
I Like Mountain Music
You're Driving Me Crazy
Take Me Out To The Ball Game
Hot Lips
*Back Home Again In Indiana
I Ain't Got Nobody
The Coat And The Pants Do All Of The Work
How Ya Gonna Keep 'Em Down On The Farm
Red Hot Fannie
*Down In Jungle Town
A Hot Dog A Blanket And You
From The Indies To The Andes In His Undies
The Martins And The Coys

CD#2
Rural Rhythm
Connie's Got Connections In Connecticut
My Wife Is On A Diet
The Guy Who Stole My Wife
Noah's Wife (Lived A Wonderful Life)
Windmill Tillie
Since We Put A Radio Out In The Henhouse
Blues (My Naughty Sweetie Gives To Me)
Let's Not And Say We Did
There'll Be Some Changes Made
My Bonnie
Dude Cowboy
When Lightnin' Struck The Coon Creek Party Line
One-Eyed Sam
She's Got A Great Big Army Of Friends
She Was A Washout In The Blackout
*The Covered Wagon Rolled Right Along
*You'd Be Surprised

*These recordings were released for the first time.

Havin' Fun With The Hoosier Hot Shots – Collector's Choice Music CCM 1034. Issued in 2003. Two CD Set. This is a reissue of Tops Records LP #L1541 with a few songs from Dot LP #DLP 25561.

Everybody Stomp – Proper Music Properbox 63. Issued in 2003, this 4 CD British set includes all the familiar Hot Shot songs but was badly butchered by editing.

The following Hoosier Hot Shot CDs are also available at the time of this writing:

The HHS in the '50s.
The HHS in the '60s.
The HSS "The Following Has Been Prerecorded."
The HHS Live In Elko.
The HHS Music From The Movies – Volume 1

The HHS Music From The Movies – Volume 2
The HHS Music From The Movies – Volume 3
The HHS Music From The Movies – 3 CD set of above titles.
The HHS Mutual Radio Show – Volume 1
The HHS Mutual Radio Show – Volume 2
The HHS Mutual Radio Show – Volume 3
The HHS Mutual Radio Show – Volume 4
The HHS Mutual Radio Show – Volume 5
The HHS Mutual Radio Show – Volume 6
The HHS Mutual Radio Show – Volume 8
The HHS Mutual Radio Show – Volume 9
The HHS Mutual Radio Show – Volume 10
The HHS 18 Mutual Radio Shows – set of above nine titles.
The National Barn Dance – Volume 1
The National Barn Dance – Volume 2
The National Barn Dance – Volume 3
The National Barn Dance – Volume 4
The National Barn Dance – CD set of above four titles
The HHS Are You Havin' Any Fun
The HHS Hoosier Stomp
The HHS Hot Lips

Listed on LPs or CDs but not found elsewhere:

After I Say I'm Sorry
Autumn Leaves
Down By The Riverside
Everyone's Hometown
Heartaches
He's Got The Whole World In His Hands
Hound Dog
Indian Love Call
Lonesome Road
Marianne
Mister Sandman
My Blue Heaven
Wabash Charleston
Washboard Stomp
(Medley) Goodnight Irene / Show Boy / Smiles

ELECTRICAL TRANSCRIPTIONS

What the heck is an electrical transcription? Even most of us who listened to radio in the 1930s and '40s and were accustomed to hearing an announcer say, "The following is an electrical transcription" or "the preceding was an electrical transcription" didn't really know. Why should we; what did it matter to the average listener?

For an excellent description of them read "Musically Electrically Transcribed!" by Walter J. Beaupre, a former radio announcer. It's online.

Basically, an ET was a 16-inch disc leased to radio stations by four different companies. They contained music, radio shows and serials, just about anything you can name that someone wanted broadcast. The fidelity was far better than you'd get from 78 rpm records that tended to be scratchy after a few plays.

Some ETs were not recorded with the same care given to a 78 that would be sold on the open market, but on the positive side, many songs not available on 78s could be heard on them. That certainly is true of the Hoosier Hot Shots. They recorded eight of the 16-inch discs for World Transcription Service's Korncert Kings series. On the following list of titles are many not found elsewhere:

A Hill Billy Wedding In June
After You've Gone
Alexander's Ragtime Band
Baby Face
Beatrice Fairfax, Tell Me What To Do
Beer Barrel Polka
Bow Wow Blues
Breezin' Along With The Breeze
Bringin' Home The Bacon From Macon
Brown Eyes Why Are You Blue?
(Medley) By The Beautiful Sea / Asleep In The Deep
Bye Bye Bessie
Bye Bye Blues

Cuddle Up A Little Closer
Do What Your Mother Did
Don't Be Tellin' Me Your Troubles
Down Home Rag
Dude Cowboy
Dummy Song
Etiquette Blues
Farewell Blues
Four Thousand Years Ago
From The Indies To The Andes In His Undies
Good, Good, Good
Goofus
He Was A Cowboy
Here Comes The Cheer Parade
Hey Mabel!
Hot Lips
How Will We Get Her Back In The Kitchen
How Ya Gonna Keep 'Em Down On The Farm
I Like Mountain Music
Ida
I'll Make A Ring Around Rosie
I'm All Ready For The Summertime
In A Little Red Barn
(Medley) In Old New York / Sidewalks Of New York
In The Summer At The Gay Seashore
Is It True What They Say About Dixie
It Ain't Gonna Rain No Mo'
It Ain't Nobody's Biz'ness What I Do
It Looks Like Rain
Let A Smile Be Your Umbrella
Look On The Bright Side
Lookie, Lookie, Lookie, Here Comes Cookie
Ma, He's Making Eyes At Me
Meet Me By The Ice House Lizzie
Meet Me Tonight In The Cow Shed
Mimi
My Little Bimbo Down On The Bamboo Isle
No Romance In Your Soul
Nobody's Sweetheart

Oh How She Lied To Me
On The West Side Of Chicago
Pretty Baby
Put On Your Slippers And Fill Up Your Pipe
Put-Put-Put
Row, Row, Row
Runnin' Wild
Rural Rhythm
San
Sentimental Gentleman From Georgia
Since We Put A Radio Out in the Henhouse
Skeedee-Waddle-Dee-Waddle-Do
Skeleton Rag
Some Of These Days
Someday's You Can't Make A Nickel
Sweet Georgia Brown
Sweet Jenny Lee
Swing Little Indians, Swing
Texas Blues
That's What I Learned In College
The Berries And The Nuts
The Coat And Pants Do All The Work But The Vest . . .
The Covered Wagon Rolled Right Along
The Fireman's Bride
The K.P. Serenade
The Latin Quarter
The Musket Came Down From The Door
The Sheik Of Araby
Them Hill-Billies Are Mountain Williams Now
There's A Hole In The Old Oaken Bucket
This Is The Chorus
Too Little, Too Late, Little Darlin'
Toot, Toot, Tootsie
Wah-Hoo!
Wait At The Gate For Me Katy
Washington & Lee Swing
What's The Good Word Mister Bluebird
When My Baby Smiles At Me
When The Grownup Ladies Act Like Babies

When Will I Know
When You Wore A Tulip
Which Came First The Chicken Or The Egg
Whispering
Who's Your Little Hoosier
Yankee Doodle Boy
You Kissed Me Once
You Must Have Been A Beautiful Baby

BIBLIOGRAPHY

American Dance Band Discography, The – Brian Rust
American Heritage History of the 1920s & 1930s
American Premium Record Guide, 6th Edition – Les Docks
Complete Entertainment Discography, The – Brian Rust
Dillinger Days, The – John Toland (Random House, 1963)
Film Encyclopedia, The – Ephraim Katz (Perigee, 1982)
Great Depression, The – Robert S. McElvaine (Times Books)
Home Country – Ernie Pyle (William Sloane Assoc., 1947
Jazz Records 1897-1942 – Brian Rust
Leonard Maltin's Movie and Video Guide
Muncie Evening Press
Muncie Morning Star
Muncie Star-Press
Pop Memories 1890-1952 – Joel Whitburn (Billboard, 1986)
Story of Ernie Pyle, The – Lee G. Miller (Viking Press, 1950)
This Fabulous Century (Time-Life Books)
WLS 1938 Barn Dance Booklet

Internet Sources

American Big Band Database
A Brief History of Union Traction Company of Indiana
Encarta Encyclopedia
Hoosier Actors
Hoosier Hot Shots Museum (hoosierhotshots.com)
IMDh
Music Electrically Transcribed! - Walter J. Beaupre
New York Times, The
Railroads of Madison County, Indiana - Roger Hensley
Soundies: A Musical History - Ray Ellis
Starr Gennett Foundation (starrgennett.org)
Wikipedia

Websites

americanheritage.com

answers.com

bbhc.org/pointswest

cmshowcase.org/halloffame

hezzie.com (to buy Hoosier Hot Shots CDs and movies)

hillbillymusic.com

hoosierhotshots.com

lum-abner.com

otrcat.com

renfrovalley.com

richsamuels.com

saw.com

scripophily.com

starpulse.com

talentondisplay.com

tribe.com

twotonbaker.com

waynet.org/gennett

wls.com

wwva.com

xroads.Virginia.edu

Other books by DICK STODGHILL

Normandy 1944 – A Young Rifleman's War

From Devout Catholic to Communist Agitator – The
Helen Lynch Story

The Rough Old Stuff – From Mike Shayne Mystery Mag.

Jack Eddy Stories – Volume 1

Jack Eddy Stories – Volume II

Midland Murders

Bearcats! – A History of Basketball at Muncie Central

Tigers! – A History of Football at Cuyahoga Falls High

Akron City Football 1892-1999 – A Complete History
See www.dickstodghill.com

---

www.ingramcontent.com/pod-product-compliance
Lightning Source LLC
LaVergne TN
LVHW011226080426
835509LV00005B/347